Living on the Road

A journey of supernatural provision,

healing, and deliverance

Debbie Hudspeth

DEDICATION

This book is dedicated to Jesus. Not only did He love me so much to die for me, but He saved me, healed me, and delivered me. Now He uses me often to lay hands on the sick so that I can see miracles happen everywhere I go. Thank you, Jesus! I am forever grateful!

Living on the Road

ACKNOWLEDGMENTS

A Special thank you to those that helped me with the editing process. Thank you, Rhonda Ellis, Dr. Kathy Fite, Ray Hunt, Sue Smit, Joy Quan and Julie Andrews.

Thanks also to my wonderful husband, Chad, and my two awesome daughters, Holly and Heidi for all their love and support.

TABLE OF CONTENTS

Living on the Road

1

HOME SWEET HOME

"There must be more. I know there is more. God, use me in a mighty way! I know there is so much more." That was my prayer as I knelt with my head on the cream colored comforter of my king-sized bed in 2005. It wasn't that I did not love my life, because I did. I felt in my spirit that more was to come and I wanted all of it. Day after day, my prayer was the same. Change was on the horizon; I did not see it coming.

At the time, I was a children's minister at a Baptist church in a small country town just north of Fort Worth, Texas. Our town did not have much to offer, only a school, three churches, a country store, and a gas station. Church was "the thing" that all the kids from the school did and I was glad to be a part of what the Lord was doing in our community.

I took the children, first through sixth graders, on outings once a month to build relationships. What fun we had! I remember one time the circus was coming to town! Not our town but one about an hour away. I received a package of free tickets in the mail. "Wow!" I thought, "This will be a great opportunity for the kids." Many had never been to the circus so I started planning the details. I would have use of two church vans plus any adults that were willing to help transport the children to the three-ring show.

The big day came. When the children were released from school, they ran toward the vans that were waiting for them outside the building. There were so many children, about 50. We loaded them into the vans. As they took their seats, I noticed a little boy standing with his mom. She decided not to let him go on the trip, but I could tell that he wanted to come with us. My heart ached for him. I saw a tear roll down his cheek as we drove away. The reason the mom was not letting her son attend the outing was because of the other children who were going. Most of the children who attended our church were from broken homes. Many of them lived with only one parent and they were often left alone at home. They had to be strong to protect themselves and they could be a bad influence on other children, at times.

As we arrived and at the *Big Top*, we unloaded the children from the vans. They started running toward the tents. With anticipation, they had big smiles as they ran to look inside the circus tent. As we got closer to the door, I felt a little out of control. Usually, I had control over the children when we went on field trips but not this day. They ran to take their seats after some bought cotton candy, snow cones, and souvenirs. As I found the section where most of them gathered to sit, I asked another adult, "Are we all here?" "I hope so," she said smiling. Living on their own, most of these independent children knew how to take care of themselves. Thankfully, they all found us as the show began. Those children and the events of that day remain a wonderful memory.

My husband, Chad, was the part-time youth minister at the same church. We lived in his hometown. He was raised in this church so he had a special love for the youth in this country town. He loved those teenagers and had a good-sized group as well.

Our life was full of ministry and loving the children in this town. We were like a mom and dad to them. We thought that we would always be there for them. One sixth grade girl stayed with us on Wednesday nights so that she could attend church. She was and still is like a daughter to us.

Each week I would visit the school at lunchtime. Being that it was a small school, all the elementary aged children ate together. I knew the majority of them and was always trying to get new ones to come to church on Wednesday nights. We used the two church vans to pick up the children. Many came without their other family members. The church became the family for many of these children.

Chad owned a business which was located thirty minutes away from where we lived. When the attacks of 9-11 happened, his business halted. We knew that God was our provider, but we had no income for several months. The church gave us some salary but not enough to survive. We had to file bankruptcy. My husband closed his business and began to try other types of work. I searched for and discovered some prayers to say in times of need. I wrote them out and said them each day, sometimes multiple times a day.

Chad's business is God's business and God's business always prospers. Chad uses God's riches wisely, judiciously, and constructively to bless himself and others. He knows the law of increase is now working, and he is open and receptive to God's wealth and bountiful increase.

Chad is richly and abundantly supplied within and without from the infinite storehouse of riches in his subconscious mind. By day and night, he is attracting more and more people who want what he has to offer. They are prospering and he is prospering. Chad's mind and heart are open to the influx (importation of abundance) of God's riches now and forevermore.

None of this was true when I started saying it. We were not prospering and no one wanted what Chad had to offer at that time. I pressed on and kept saying these words. God spoke in the very beginning of creation and THEN things came to be. I was speaking aloud these words with hope that our situation would change quickly. I was calling those things that were not as though they were (Romans 4:17).

There was no change, at least none that I could see right then. But the Bible says, "Death and life are in the power of the tongue, and those who live it will eat its fruits" (Proverbs 18:21). I continued to walk by faith and not by what I could see, think, or feel. I kept trusting God and speaking life.

Things became worse. We were at a point that something had to change. I logged on the Internet one night and started looking for a children's ministry job in a bigger church. I did this to push Chad to find a different job, but I did not tell him that at the time. I remember one night he asked me what I was doing on the computer. I told him that I was looking for a job. "What about Alabama, would you want to live there? There is an opening at a church that looks really good," I called to him from the other room. My husband thought I was crazy looking for a job outside of Texas. We were both born in Texas. We grew up in Texas. Our families lived in Texas. We lived in Texas, and Chad said that we would never leave Texas. However, night after night, I looked for jobs on the computer and talked about how great I thought these churches were. In reality, I never intended to move anywhere.

I had been a stay-at-home mom from the time I had my first little blessing, Holly, who was now in first grade. We were also blessed with another adorable girl, Heidi. She was in half-day Pre-K which freed me to do my church work. Our girls spent a lot of time at the church while Chad and I worked with the children and youth.

We kept busy with many outreach activities for the children and youth in the town. Looking back, there were almost too many activities. Our weekends were filled with lock-ins, game nights, Super Bowl parties, ice skating, roller skating, trips to concerts, picnics, inflatables, etc. It was a great season, and we were watching God turn lives around through the hearts of the children and youth. Little did we know that it would soon be ending, as every season does.

2

THE SHIFT

As the days passed, Chad's attitude about moving from Texas was slowly changing. Hurricane Katrina had recently hit Louisiana. One of his friends was working there and called Chad to tell him about some construction work that was available there. On New Year's Day, 2006, we planned a trip to see for ourselves what job opportunities were available. Chad decided that if I was looking for work out-of-state, he could consider it as well.

We were not sure what to expect but we traveled to Louisiana in faith that God would lead us. The devastation was still widespread throughout New Orleans. Entire communities were still without electricity and FEMA trailers were at nearly every house. There was an almost tangible sadness hovering over the land and the people. The locals were still talking about the disaster on a daily basis. Doors of opportunity started to open, and Chad talked with a man about getting a job. The opportunities for work seemed good and we were slowly accepting the fact that we would be moving due to financial reasons. We decided to go for it and leave the great state of Texas. We put our house on the market and began to pack.

The scripture that God laid on my heart was Ephesians 3:20 which states "Now to Him who is able to do exceedingly abundantly above all that we ask or think, according to the power that works in us." Our first hotel room in Louisiana was number 320. I do not believe in coincidence so I was certain that God was confirming the verse I was standing on. We left the hotel in the morning because we wanted to stay closer to New Orleans. However, due to all the construction and devastation, there were no hotels open. We had to return to the same hotel which was now hours away. Once we got there, they gave us the same room 320 which confirmed that we were on the right path.

While we traveled back to Texas, we made plans for Chad to move to Louisiana in two weeks. I would stay in Texas and keep our two girls in school until our house sold. We bought the house seven years earlier and totally remodeled it. We thought the house would sell quickly and our family would be reunited. On the drive back, the Lord laid three people on my heart to call and tell that we were moving. All three of those people contacted me within two days of our return to Texas. They called me before I had a chance to call them. God was in this.

Chad was home for about two weeks when we informed the church that we would be leaving. There was not a dry eye that night as I told the children and Chad shared with the youth that we were moving out of state. I still remember walking outside as we were leaving the church and seeing tears falling from the children. It was one of the most difficult partings in my life. I thought this was going to be the hardest part of moving and it was hard! However, the hardest part was yet to come.

At this point, Chad ran an advertising business that he had created. We needed cash fast, and the Lord led a young man to call him about buying his business. Within a few days, he paid us several thousand dollars and the deal was done. It was a *God thing* because we needed some money to carry us over before his paychecks from the new job in Louisiana would begin. We had past bills that needed to be paid with this money. We could feel God's hand working. We were sure that we were headed in the right direction.

Chad recruited a friend who had an RV (recreation vehicle) to travel to Louisiana to work with him. It was great how God sends His people out two by two. I felt better knowing that Chad was not alone. The two men packed up and headed out on Saturday morning. As they drove off, I remember laughing saying, "Just send the money." Our supply of cash was next to nothing.

My children continued as normal in school, but it was more challenging for me. People started coming out of the woodwork when they found out we were moving. They wanted to come by, call, and take me to lunch "one more time" before we left. It was overwhelming.

When Chad first left, I was okay. I spent the evenings painting the house and watching a Beth Moore DVD series. It kept me busy. Hearing the Word of God is always a good thing to do. I spoke the Word of God each day over our finances and spent time praising the Lord with worship music. I was renewing my mind each day, knowing the Lord was taking good care of me.

After only a few weeks, the newness began wearing off and my tears started to fall. As I tucked in my oldest child into bed one evening, I could tell she was missing her daddy. I was missing him as well. We started crying together at bedtime each night. How much longer could this continue? Why was I crying like this? I am not a person who cries this much. When God when? How God how? I cannot do this for very long.

The stress began to fall over our family, especially me. I had the pressure of getting the house ready to sell, packing, being a single parent while my husband was away, and leaving the community, our family, and the church. Our pastor, a dear friend of mine, asked me to step down as the children's minister and train another leader. That was painful because my involvement with the children and ministry helped get my mind off my current situation; but I did as he requested.

Chad flew home every few weeks to visit. It was great to see him. We could not get enough of him while he was home. One time in particular, when he came home, I cried the entire weekend. I would just look at him and cry, and he would ask, "Why are you crying? I am here." I was not sure then but looking back, it was clear that I was depressed.

He was off again and I was alone. One day the phone rang non-stop from people in the community calling to say their goodbyes. I put on some headphones playing praise music while I lay on the floor. This lifestyle was exhausting me. "How much more, God?" I thought. I was getting weaker and weaker. For several years, I suffered with back issues and was having a hard time getting around. I felt like I was carrying around a large elephant from the weight of all that I had to do.

A friend called me one day and told me about 1 Peter 5:7 which says, "Cast all your care upon Him, for He cares for you." Then, she told me to write down all the things that I was worrying about, each on its own piece of paper, wad them up, and keep them on my desk as a reminder that God has these in His hands. I did it. I listed all my worries: money for food and bills, Chad being gone, house to sell, back pain, upset relatives, my girls' sadness, etc. I wrote them out and prayed over each one "casting it before the Lord." I left the notes on my desk as a reminder. I prayed each time I walked by the desk. When Holly came home from school that day, she put the notes in the trash can. I thought that was the perfect place for all my worries to go. I knew God was with me and helping me even though I could not see any change yet.

Things became worse for me the longer Chad stayed away. The back pain became so severe that I could hardly walk. I had friends come over to vacuum my house and clean up when I was having a house showing. One afternoon, Holly became sick and she threw up, but I could not get on the floor to clean up the mess. How humbling it was to not be able to care for my children. I called my sweet neighbor and she came right over. My sister called at one point and wanted to take Heidi for a week. I gladly let her go, feeling as though I could not take care of her.

One day a good friend came over and sat down with me. Her husband was a pilot and she was used to being apart from him. She told me that it was not good for Chad and me to be apart. I needed to leave the house and head to Louisiana to be with him. She could tell that I had been struggling more and more as each week passed.

Thankfully, Chad agreed. After living apart for three months, we loaded up in our van and left Texas during spring break March 2006. The drive was wonderful because we were all together. We were cramped in the van. There was no foot room because we had so much stuff. We did not care. We were together and that was all that mattered to us.

3

ONLY 10 DAYS?

Upon arrival in Mandeville, Louisiana, we settled into a RV that we borrowed. It was a 5th Wheel with only one bedroom. The girls were young and small. They slept on either side of the bed on the floor in an extremely narrow space. They did not care because their mom and dad were close by and that was more than enough for them. Fortunately, we had two weeks off for Spring Break before school started. During that time, I enrolled Holly in school, bought her new uniforms, and accepted a job at a day care, which Heidi would be attending. We were ready to settle down and get involved in the community. Chad had found an awesome church that we were looking forward to attending on Sunday.

During the days, the girls and I would find nearby parks. I

was amazed to see different flowers and trees that we did not have in Texas. They were blooming because it was springtime. It was so beautiful. At night, after dinner, we would play cards and laugh. To be together again was amazing. Little did I know, things would be changing rather quickly...again!

I still sensed heaviness amongst the people in the city of Mandeville. Many were still living in FEMA trailers parked in their own driveway. Everywhere we traveled, people spoke of the storm and the devastation that was still in plain view even though it happened seven months earlier. Trees were still down in some places, buildings ripped to pieces and downed signs still lined the sides of the road. Many transformations had taken place but it could possibly be years before the town was totally renovated.

Chad found a great church since he had been working in the area for the past three months. The teaching was good but the children's area was over the top. They had an indoor playground including a tunnel system that made McDonald's Play Place look elementary. It was a great time for fellowship as all the parents hung around the playground after church waiting for their children to pop out of the brightly colored tunnels. What are the reasons that we attend church? Is it so that our children will have a wonderful time playing? It is great to have fun activities for children to do but more importantly to learn about the amazing stories of the Bible.

One day the girls and I were out at a park when Chad called. He told me that his company wanted him to move to Missouri the following week. We did not know that this company traveled when we accepted the position. The idea of moving again hit me hard. "What about the school, the uniforms, and my new job, which was supposed to start the following Monday?" These thoughts and more began running through my head. I was moving with my husband no matter what. There was no way I was going to stay in Louisiana apart from him. "Let's go!" I told him. We packed up and headed out over the weekend after being in Louisiana only ten days.

"Oh, I will let you call all the family and let them know of this change," I told him jokingly as we hit the road. It was hard enough for them to see us leave Texas but now to move again after only 10 days in Louisiana? He called his side of the family, and I called mine. All were shocked, of course, but they were glad to see us leaving Louisiana because of the devastation still present from Hurricane Katrina. We did not know what to expect, but we knew God was leading us to a new and exciting place. Once again, we packed up everything we owned into my van and his truck and took to the road. This was only the beginning. I had no idea what awaited our family.

At times in our life, faith in God is needed. When Abram was 75 years old, the Lord told him to leave his country, his family, and everything that made him feel comfortable and go to a land that God would show him (Genesis 12:1-9). Abram was okay with that scene. It is tough to move and leave everything that you know.

While living a life trusting the Lord, it does not always make sense. We were beginning a spiritual journey but we did not know it. Remember those prayers that I mentioned in the beginning of this book? "God, I know there is more. Show me more. I know there is more to this Christian walk. Show it to me." God was about to open our eyes to "the more." He was going to reveal the Bible to us in a whole new light, a way in which we had not seen before.

I was raised in church. We attended most Sundays when we were not out on the lake. Sadly, I did not learn anything about the Bible. We were not encouraged to read our Bible or bring it to church. There was a red Bible in our pew but we rarely opened it during the service.

In Junior High, I remember going through confirmation class. I was not sure what was "confirmed" but I was excited about having a lock-in at the church with all my friends! I do not remember making a decision to follow Jesus as it says in Romans 10:9-10 "If you confess with your mouth the Lord Jesus and believe in your heart that God raised Him from the dead, you will be saved. For with the heart one believes unto righteousness, and with the mouth confession is made unto salvation." That is the only way to get into heaven and after spending 18 years at that church, no one ever explained that to me. Thankfully, I attended a summer camp with a church down the street. That is where I gave my heart to Jesus and started my walk as a new believer.

One Sunday I tried really hard to understand our pastor. I could not. It was so confusing. When I got in the car I was hoping that my parents would explain what he was talking about. "Wow, that was a good sermon today," I said trying to get an explanation. My parents simply replied, "Oh yea, it was good."

I did not like church growing up. It was boring. We stood

up at certain times, sang certain songs each week and went forward for communion once a month to kneel in front of the entire church. I liked that day because I could see who was there but did not understand the meaning of communion.

Jesus is speaking and is very clear when He says "He who believes in Me, the works that I do he will do also; and greater works than these he will do, because I go to My Father" (John 14:12). I have all authority according to Matthew 28:18 that Jesus left for me when he rose from the dead. Yet, because of the lack of knowledge in my hometown church and churches all over the world today, people are being destroyed: in marriages, health, and finances because they have not been taught the things of the Bible.

Thankfully, our eyes were opened to the "MORE" in Columbia, Missouri, by a pastor who was not afraid to speak the truth of the Word of God. One of the names of Jesus is "Truth." There is power when you speak the truth out.

It is so crucial where you are attending church. In Acts 17:11 there is a group of people called the Bereans. The Bible tells how they would "examine the Scriptures every day to see if what Paul said was true." They did not merely accept what he was saying; they studied. Be like the Bereans and examine the Word of God. Study it often and see for yourself what it says.

4

DEMARET STREET

All that we had was in our truck and minivan as we headed north to Missouri. We had no idea where we were going to live or the adventures that lay ahead of us. Chad had two days to travel and then had to be at work. So, we acted quickly. Our money supply was still very low so he could not miss a day of work.

We made it in one full day of driving. We stayed in a hotel for the night in the college town of Columbia, Missouri, our new home. I got a newspaper and started calling around to find a place to live. We had less than one day to find a place and move in. We found a duplex that was vacant on both sides. They had just replaced the carpet, which was great because we would be sleeping on the floor on airbeds. We signed the lease, unloaded the truck and Chad left for work.

I asked the landlord how to pronounce the name of the street. "Demerit," he said. I should have thought about that a little longer. From the direction that we traveled to the duplex, we did not realize that we were in the lowest of low housing. A demerit is a mark against you, and these people had been marked against. After the school buses dropped off the kids and the parents came home, it was scary. We stayed inside at night, uncertain of the safety of our neighborhood.

Try to imagine our little duplex. Our living room furniture consisted of camping chairs with Chad's toolbox as our coffee table. The computer was on the floor along with the TV. In the bedrooms we had airbeds and sleeping bags. I bought a dresser at a garage sale for $7.00 that had a mirror. On the walls we taped colored pieces of paper for decoration and to help reduce the echoing sounds that came from talking in a room with no furniture. I wrote scriptures on some of the papers and taped others in a design on the wall. It was very humbling. Needless to say, I was fine with living there, but I was not inviting anyone over to see where we were living.

Chad worked long hours. He would get home after dark each night. I stayed home with Heidi while Holly went to an awesome art school that she grew to love. Chad and I would stay up late working on paperwork for his job. He was doing great, and I wanted to help out any way that I could. One night as we were working, I saw a flashing light outside our window. We looked out and were shocked to see it was an MRAP (Mine-Resistant Ambush Protected) and several police vehicles. We heard some gunshots and ran for the hall. While we were kneeling there, Chad said, "You picked this place!" "What? You helped me find it! You were with me!" I replied. We were scared and not sure what was happening at the time. I wanted to move but we were unsure where to go that would be safer. We did not have the money to keep moving around. We watched the news the next night and found out that there had been a murder right across the street from us. As we prayed that night, we thanked God for our protection (Psalm 91:8-10).

On Sunday, we went to a large church that we found on the Internet with tons of activities for the children and young families. They were in a building project which meant they were growing. We decided to stay and dropped the girls off at their classes and Chad and I made our way to the sanctuary. Near the door was a buffet of different coffee drinks. It was all free and everyone had a coffee cup. We don't drink coffee so we took our seats.

The worship music started and the lights went down. It was as if we were at a concert. Then I noticed no one was singing the worship songs. They were just watching and sipping on their drinks. The man in front of me got up and went to get a refill. The message was good but lacked "meat". I was hungry for God and needed more. As we walked out, I noticed that I was the only one with a Bible. Something was wrong with that picture. Coffee is not bad but should it replace the Bible in church? The service seemed like an item to check off your Sunday list. I wanted an encounter with the Lord. Before we got to the car, we decided that this church was not for us.

After searching for several weeks, we found an outstanding church and the Bible came alive to us. We began to learn things that seemed so simple but were never taught before. We learned how there is power of life and death in the tongue (Proverbs 18:21) and by speaking out the Word of God; you can change your situation. I was still making the confessions about Chad and his business but now we were taking it to a whole new level by speaking scriptures over our current situation. Change is what we needed so we wrote out some scriptures for our finances, and we both started speaking the Word out loud daily. Here is what we would say:

I respect the Lord, and He will instruct me in the way chosen. I will spend my days in prosperity and my descendants will inherit the land. Psalm 25:12-13

The Lord inhabits the praises of His people. I meditate on the Word of God day and night. Then I am becoming prosperous and successful. Joshua 1:8

*He who trusts in the Lord will prosper.
I trust in the Lord and will prosper. Proverbs 28:25*

I remember the Lord, it is He who gives me the power to create wealth. God prospers me abundantly in all the work of my hands. Deuteronomy 8:18, 30:9

The Lord blesses me and surrounds me with favor as with a shield. Psalm 5:12

I am made rich in every way so I can be generous on every occasion. 2 Corinthians 9:11

Beloved, I wish above all else that you prosper and be in health even as your soul prospers. 3 John 1:2

Within two weeks, our finances began to change. Chad's income doubled for the next several years after we started confessing the Word of God over our situation. The Word works but you have to "work" it by speaking it out of your mouth and believing it. Jeremiah 23:29 says "Is not My word like a fire?" says the Lord, "And like a hammer that breaks rock in pieces?" A hammer is of no use unless it is picked up. You need to speak it out to see results.

At the church, people would give testimonies of God's goodness. There were healings and miracles spoken about which I never heard before. There was an infant that had something wrong with her eyes and after the church prayed, she was totally healed. All the infection and blindness disappeared. I was so interested in that. Could it really be that God still heals? Why had I not heard of this at my former church? They even had a time for healing during the service. Four people (prayer team) would go down front and others would come to them who needed prayer at the end of the church service. I watched so closely, almost like the spiritual police, as to what was happening in this church. Regular people were praying for other people and miracles were happening. Wow! This was so cool! I wanted to do that but had no idea how to stand in their shoes.

One of the couples on the prayer team invited us over to her house for dinner. This was awesome because I wanted to know their secrets for praying. Guess what I found out? There were no secrets. They were doing what the Bible says to do. "Lay hands on the sick, and they will recover" (Mark 16:17-19). They believed the Bible and did it. We ended up going often to their house. I loved the nights we would spend talking about the Lord. They would tell stories that captivated my attention and made me hunger for more of Jesus.

Day after day, we stood on the Word of God. With each word spoken, seeds were being sown. It takes a while to see the harvest. There were days we thought the harvest would never come but it was under the surface. Things were moving and changing, yet we could not see them. When you speak the Word of God, things *have* to change.

I found a beautiful lake to walk around. In the mornings, I would go there to walk with the Lord, praying about the situation that we were in. I would focus on Him and His Word while I was walking instead of my current living conditions. The Bible says to set your mind on things above and to renew your mind with His Word. (Colossians 3:2, Romans 12:2) During this time, I was clinging to Jesus like never before; He was all that we had.

Twelve weeks in Columbia, Missouri, and it was time to move again because of Chad's job. I was glad to move but sad to leave the church and the friendships that we had started. God is so good to bless us with people who love Him and who loved us while we were there. They will forever be in our hearts. We learned so much about confessing the Word over our circumstances.

With the van loaded down once more, we hit the road in the summer heat. This time, the girls and I were going back to Texas while Chad was heading to Alabama to work. Our home in Texas finally sold. I was going to sell our things that were still in the house and Chad would come back for the closing.

When we arrived back in Texas, my girls visited family and friends while I tackled my house once again. I decided to have a moving sale to sell almost everything and I was so blessed to have so much help from my friends and family that loved and missed us. Chad flew in to move a few things into storage and then we were off again, this time, living in Alabama.

We moved out to northern Alabama with just a few weeks of summer left. All this moving around was getting too hard so we decided to purchase an RV to make moving easier. Once in Alabama, the search was on to quickly find an RV while we lived in an extended stay hotel. We found one and bought it but after only a week, we realized that it was way too small. We started our search again and found one a little bigger. Even though it only had a 5-gallon hot water heater, we bought it and the simple life began!

Our financial situation had improved greatly. We sold our home in Texas with a fair amount of equity and the Lord began to prosper us. Chad was excelling in his job as we continued to confess the Word of God over our situation.

5

THE SIMPLE LIFE

Decatur, Alabama, was to be our new home for now. I was raised in central Texas and was used to the Southern drawl, but the accent here was a little extreme. Many times I would just listen to the townspeople speaking and think, "Do they really talk this way?" It was different, but we loved the kindness of the people.

Our RV Park was awesome and clean. We had tall pine trees and a bike trail around the lake. There was a small but nice school right around the corner. We had about a week to enroll before school started. Holly was in 2nd grade and Heidi was starting Kindergarten.

At night, I would make dinner and then we would go on a

family bike ride before coming back to eat. Heidi learned how to ride her bike with no training wheels in that RV Park. I can still remember her going all the way to the curve, stopping and walking her bike around the corner, and then getting back on it. Those curves were tricky for her. Not many people could say that they learned how to ride their bike in an RV park, but we were not a normal family and that was okay with us.

One night, I was sitting outside by a campfire and a friendly lady came walking by. She invited me to the Dulcimer gathering inside one of the meeting rooms in the RV Park. I had no idea what a Dulcimer was and she explained that it was mountain music. All I could recall was that old song "Oh play me some mountain music like grandma and grandpa used to play" by the band Alabama. I always wanted to know what mountain music was so I talked Holly into going with me. As we walked into the room, I noticed many older people and only a few my age. There was a circle of people with Dulcimer instruments on their laps. One person would call out a song and the rest would strum along. Some would sing, others would just play, and all had a great time. It was down-home music for sure, pickin' and grinnin'.

Not long after we settled into school, Chad decided to find a home for sale that needed to be fixed up. Off season for his job was coming, and he thought it would be a good idea for us to fix up a home to live in and later sell. I was not for this at all. I was really happy in the camper. It was small, manageable, and easy to clean. Everyone had a bed; there was a kitchen table and a couch. Having a couch to sit on was a blessing. To encourage my husband, I went along with the idea and started spending my days looking at houses with different realtors.

Meanwhile, it took us about three Sundays of looking before we found a church. It was on fire! By now, it was getting easier to walk into a church and tell if that was where God was leading us. It was always unanimous between Chad and me and our daughters when selecting a church. We would all be in agreement if this was the fit for us. At this point, I was finding myself more reserved. I really did not want to get close to the people at this church, because I knew that I would be moving. It hurts too much to keep doing that. So, I became a pew hugger for a while, focusing on Jesus. God knows what is best for us. We were created for relationships. There was the cutest couple that sat near us. During the greeting time, we became friends and eventually started going to lunch together with their family. They also moved around a lot so we were a perfect fit for each other.

Our search for a house ended after two months. We bought a house that was in really good shape but needed major updating. We went in full force tearing out walls, putting up new walls, ripping out the carpet, and painting every room. We recruited two college-age men from our church that helped us on a regular basis. We worked hard on the house for three months. We finally parked our RV in the back yard and moved in. We brought our keepsakes out of storage from Texas, bought some furniture, and turned this house into our new home. What we were wanting was to settle down and put some roots down. This was our third state in only five months and we were ready to get off the road. You see, sometimes we try to stop the journey that we are on more quickly than what

God has planned. It was not the time for us to settle down even though the girls were in school and I wanted to feel the comfort of having a home once again. I still needed to learn how to trust God for my place in life. God's plans for our family are perfect.

I wonder how many times Abraham tried to stop on his journey to make a new home for his family but he kept going until he knew it was time to stop. We were trying to rush God's plan and stay in Alabama. I really liked it here but the place was not right. I even interviewed for a job but did not get it. No, it was not God's plan.

Our church had many activities where you could get "plugged in." There was one called Adopt-a-Block that our family got involved with. We went out to the same block once a month to pick up trash and visit with the homeowners. Then we invited them to the church to receive free clothing and food. It is a great way to show the love of Jesus one block at a time. When the families came to the church, I started having some activities for the children while their parents attended the meeting and received their free supplies. It was so good to work with these children. We played on the playground, did arts and crafts and I told Bible stories. I was becoming more and more involved and then it happened. My husband informed me that it was time to move again. "Oh, no!" I thought because there was so much for me to do here. "What about these kids? Who will take over?" My husband and I agreed that he would go out-of-state to work while the girls finished the year in school. Then, we would join him. That gave me more time with the children at the church.

As the school year ended, we decided to keep the house and return in the fall. The desire was still in us to have a "home" and be plugged in somewhere. This time, the move was much different. We were used to being in the south and now we were headed north, to Uniontown, Ohio. We loaded the RV and headed out, packing all of our warm clothes.

After only six weeks in Ohio, we knew that we were going to stay longer due to the workload. We decided to put the freshly remodeled house in Alabama for sale and in 29 days, we had a good offer. Within a few weeks, we were moved out and packed our possessions in storage. Away to Ohio we traveled for the next adventures awaiting our family.

6

OHIO

Ohio was beautiful. The grass was greener than any I had ever seen. The air was cool all the time and the rolling hills were breathtaking. The campground where we lived was really wonderful. It included a water park and a really nice putt-putt golf course. We enjoyed our summer and spent a lot of our time at the library where they had wonderful activities for kids and families. One of the greatest activities we learned about is Letterboxing. It is a national treasure hunt with clues online to hidden boxes all over the world. We had some sweet friends that would venture out with us as we saw some amazing parts of Ohio that otherwise we would not have seen. Oh, what fun we had!

As the summer was winding down, Chad told me one night that he would like me to homeschool the children. Really, me? Homeschool in a small camper? Could that really happen? As much as I loved my girls, I liked some time away from them. I used to teach in a public school and made fun of homeschooled children. Some of them seemed socially disconnected and I did not want our children to fit into that category. I would have to pray about this and see.

As I sought the Lord, He assured me that this was the right thing to do for now. I found a homeschool book fair and went to check it out. As I walked in and started looking at all the curriculum, I was overwhelmed. How would I know what to buy? Did I need every book they offered? I finally went and sat against the wall and watched the other people. For about ten minutes I observed others to see if they had "confusion" written on their faces. They did not. These moms were pros. They walked in, flipped through the books and placed their orders. Even the moms that were new had done all their research online and acted like they were pros. I eventually ordered and left, feeling unsure if I could make it through an entire year. Surely, this lifestyle would end soon and I could put my kids back in school.

There was a lot of time for seeking the Lord during this season of my life. I remember one day asking the Lord if I could do something for Him at the church. He told me that this was a season of rest for me. I thought that I had been resting ever since we got on the road. I was not happy with that so I looked into helping at the church. The church required that you attend two membership classes that were several months apart before helping in any area. I agree that bigger churches need a way to sift through people in order to get to know them first before letting them work in their church. So, with a shut door, I went to church to worship and learn the Word, and that I did!

Our church had some outstanding visiting ministers that came for a week-long conference. I went every night to learn more from the Word of God. One night when I picked up my girls from the childcare, I noticed my oldest daughter, who was 8 years old, was laughing more than usual. I asked her why she was so happy and she said that someone had prayed for her at the conference. She began to have a lot of energy and started running around the gym. The more she told me about the night, the more she began to laugh until she was belly laughing non-stop. What I did not understand at the time was that the Holy Spirit touched her that night in the kids program. She received holy laughter or "drunk" in the spirit, as some would call it. When you are ready for "more" of God, you will receive it, whether you understand it or not.

As I planned for the year, I was getting more excited about teaching. Before my children were born, I taught children in first grade at a public school. As I flipped through the pages of the new books that just came in the mail, I greatly anticipated the year. We could start when we wanted each morning and end around lunchtime; things were sounding good.

The first day of school came, and my girls did well. They completed all their work and we were finished around lunchtime, which was good because I had to clear all the books from the table in order to serve lunch in our booth. Camper life had its perks but extra space was not one of them.

We joined the YMCA because they had an indoor pool. I knew the weather was going to get cold and we needed some exercise. They had some homeschool classes there so we joined those as well. One of them was a rocket class and the girls created rockets and then blasted them off outside. It was a chilly 34 degrees the day they shot them off. We were bundled up as we watched the rockets go higher than we thought they could. It was a great experience!

One day while we were swimming at the YMCA, we met another family: a mom and her two girls. I told the Lord earlier that I was not going to make any friends while I was here because it was too hard to leave. So, I was not overly friendly. However, she was. She came and sat by me and began talking to me about the girls. She ended up giving me her phone number and told me to call if I needed to know anything about the area. We talked back and forth on the phone and she invited us over to her house for sledding and hot chocolate. It was a fun invitation since we never experienced that in Texas. God always provides for us.

We joined a homeschool group that went on field trips about once a month. We went to some really cool places. I had my guard up again and did not want to make any new friends because I knew that we would be moving again. We went to a play in a neighboring town about thirty minutes away. We did not sit with our homeschool group. We sat alone. Sure enough, the family from the YMCA was sitting right in front of us. My girls noticed them and we moved our seats to sit with them. Afterwards, we went to Chick-fil-A to play and eat together.

God created us for relationships. He wants us to have a relationship with Him and with others. He tells us in his Word that we are to love others and carry each other's burdens (John 13:34, Galatians 6:2). You can't do that if you have no friends at all, which is what I was trying to do. It was wrong.

One of our favorite things to do while in Ohio was to visit the Amish community. The rolling green hills were gorgeous with the rows of crops planted by each family. Their houses were loaded with beautiful flowers of every color and they always had a garden outside the kitchen. You could see the clothes hung out to dry and we got excited when we passed each Amish buggy.

The Amish had a cheese factory that we visited often. We fell in love with their varieties of cheese, especially their chocolate cheese that tasted like fudge. Each time we had our family come for a visit, we would take them there because you could sample the cheese. There were over a hundred different flavors; it was like going to a buffet.

Our neighbors at the RV Park were in there 70's. They were "snowbirds" and lived there only part of the year. They traveled to Florida for the winter. When we first arrived, she came over to let us know that no children lived in that section of the park because they wanted to keep the noise down. I assured her that we would be quiet. My children were shocked and did not feel welcome there but I told them that we are going to love our neighbors. "Soon they will see Jesus in us, and they will love us back," I confidently said. That is exactly what happened. When you show others the unconditional love of Jesus, they can't help but see that there is something different about you. The last day that we saw them they both had tears in their eyes as they waved good-bye. We keep in touch by email. Now they are attending a church regularly and seek God more as they get to the end of their lives.

We always vacationed near where we were living. So when my mom, sister, and her children flew up, we took a road trip to Niagara Falls, Canada. It was a short, seven-hour drive; well worth it. The falls were so magnificent. We went on every tour offered and saw the falls from every angle. We rode a boat out near the falls, went into the tunnel behind the falls, followed the sidewalk down from the falls, and rode the Ferris wheel to see the falls from the sky. There was a fee for all of that, but we discovered that the BEST view was just standing at the top. While we were there, we saw a full, beautiful, double rainbow. Wow! I had never seen such a sight before. God's beauty is so amazing.

7

OUR LONGEST STAY

In March 2008, we headed to Franklin, Kentucky, where we invested in an RV park with some friends from Chad's work. We lived in our RV for a month as we fixed up the park. We loved living in Kentucky. The people there are so kind. My girls spent their days roaming around the park and riding on the golf cart while Chad and I worked on some renovations. The RV Park we purchased was really nice but needed some fixing up in a few areas. We wanted to stay longer but work was calling in Georgia.

We moved to Madison, Georgia, where we lived for one year. Madison is known as the "The Prettiest Small Town in America" with nearly 100 antebellum homes that have been restored. Madison was named after President James Madison and was spared from burning during Sherman's March to the Sea. Even though the town was charming, we stayed in the most run down RV Park we have ever been in. Being the only park around, it was packed with RV's even though it needed a lot of repairs. It was located in a rural, countryside setting with beautiful scenery. We parked near the tall forest trees in the very back where it was peaceful and quiet. We were still homeschooling and had no regrets. The girls spent a lot of time playing outside near the forest. On the weekends, my girls would play with other children staying in the park but overall, they were happy they had each other to play with all the time.

The Lord continued increasing our finances. Chad was promoted to General Manager at his job and our finances were turning around. Those seeds of faith that we had spoken were sprouting and we were seeing the fruit of the scriptures that we had faithfully spoken.

In Madison, we found a great church. They asked me to be the Children's Minister while we were there. We became good friends with the pastor and his family and joined their homeschool group. We were blessed to make so many great friends; more than any other time while living on the road. It was a special year sharing life together. We continue to call them "friends" while we were living on the road.

The Bible continued to speak to me like never before. As I read and mediated on the scriptures, the words would ring in my mind. If Jesus is the same, yesterday, today and forever as it tells in Hebrews 13:8 why do we not live with the miracles that he did? Is healing for today?

Homeschooling had its ups and downs. There were days that the girls and I needed to be separated because we were in too close of quarters. It was a challenge to live in an RV. We traded our small camper for a 40-foot bumper-pull RV that gave us more room. It had a fireplace and a washer and dryer. Never again will I complain about washing and putting up clothes. After you have spent years in a laundromat washing clothes, you will feel the same way. Laundromats are very hot and not very clean. My girls and I had been using them once a week for three years. So, when we found out that our new RV had a washer and a dryer, we were thrilled! I did not mind that I could not run them both at the same time because of the amp pull. I washed one or two extra small loads every day which was enough to keep us away from the laundromat.

While living on the road, I continuously suffered from back pain. It would come and go every couple of weeks; but when it came, it was severe. I would have to put my life on hold and do nothing for several days. I would spend the days on the couch with ice packs and have my kids help out more than they wanted to. I also had heaviness on me that made me really weak. I kept praying against that as well. Soon, things would unexpectedly change.

Chronic pain is not fun. The pain in my lower back was so intense, I had a hard time breathing when I bent over. The motion of picking up something brought extreme pain. I suffered from this condition for about 20 years. I adapted my life around it. I honestly never considered that I could be healed of it.

Sleeping was a challenge. No bed would allow me to sleep

for an entire night without getting up with back pain. At this point, I could only sleep on an air mattress. Each time we took a trip, I would bring my airbed, sheets, and blankets. This became extremely inconvenient for me.

Sleep is so important to our health. When we sleep our body restores itself. It keeps the immune system strong and reduces stress. Thankfully, we serve a God who does not sleep or slumber (Psalm 121:4). He never tires out and is always available for us.

Why do we put up with pain? It is NOT from God. "Surely He has borne our griefs and carried away our sorrows; yet we esteemed Him stricken, smitten by God, and afflicted. But He was wounded for our transgressions, He was bruised for our iniquities; the chastisement for our peace was upon Him, and by His stripes we are healed (Isaiah 53:4-5).

Why is it that so many Christians do not have this revelation? They are not walking in the truth that Jesus still heals today. He is the same yesterday, today, and forever (Hebrews 13:8). It is time to wake up and walk in the supernatural. Jesus is coming back for a glorious church, without spot or wrinkle, but we are to be holy and without blemish (Ephesians 5:27). The church today looks just like the world: no victory in finances, divorce rate is the same, same sicknesses and diseases, and lips that speak death instead of life. (Deuteronomy 30:19). This needs to change.

After spending 12 months in beautiful historic Madison, Georgia, we were moving once again. We had a going away party with our closest friends. Since we became so involved in the homeschool group and the church, not only did my husband and I establish friendships, but my girls did too. We were on to the next phase of learning and adventuring with God.

8

ARKANSAS

For two years, my oldest daughter, Holly, asked for a dog. Finally, my husband agreed. The day after we moved to Arkansas in September 2009, we got a six-week-old puppy, a Yorkshire Terrier and a great addition to our family. We named her Madison after our great stay in Madison, Georgia.

Our days were now spent training our puppy. The girls took a puppy training class at the local pet store to learn how to train her. Madison is a traveling dog and goes wherever we go. She likes to be near us, which is good for her because she did not have to walk very far in the camper to be close to us. She was so small in the beginning that she could crawl under the doors when they were shut. (Camper doors are raised more than normal doors in a house.) It did not take long before she figured out that she could sneak under them. What joy she has brought to our family.

Chad was approached by an investor and after much prayer, he left the company he had been working for and traveling with for the past three years and started his own company. He continued to work in the same field with the investor and God greatly blessed us.

We visited a church once we got settled near Little Rock. It was a good church but it was not right for us. They had a great children's program, new church building, tons of activities but something was missing. The power of God was not there. At that point, I really did not know what I was searching for, but I was certain this church did not have it. There is freedom in the spirit and some churches quench the Holy Spirit. Having visited so many churches while living on the road, my husband and I can sense it with only one visit to a new church.

Another church had been recommended to us, but I did not want to go because the pastors were much older than what I was used to. We went anyway. That particular day, we had about 14 people coming with us from Chad's work. As we found our seat, Chad was texting them because some were lost and others did not know where to take their children during the church service. I decided that I would just focus on Jesus as the worship started.

That morning I asked the Lord to remove all weakness from me. I was so tired and had heaviness on me. At times, it was hard to stay awake to homeschool my girls. I felt exhausted everyday. Before church, I was confessing the scripture, "I am strong in the Lord and in the power of His might" (Ephesians 6:10).

Being that it was our first time to the church, I did not know the pastor. During the praise music, he called people down that had a feeling of weakness. I knew that he was talking to me. I did not even tell Chad that I was going down, I just went. He told us to lift our hands and praise the Lord. I still had not seen the pastor or knew where he was; I could only hear his voice. As I praised the Lord with my eyes closed, the pastor touched me lightly. Immediately, this power came over me, my knees buckled and down to the floor I fell.

While I was there, an extreme peace came over me. I asked the Lord to heal the weakness that I was feeling, and He spoke to me. It was not an audible voice but an inner knowing. He said, "I will do my part and you do yours." Oh, I had a part? I really did not want a part. I wanted God to touch me and totally heal my body. It felt like something heavy was laying on me while I was on the floor. I finally opened my eyes, and a man helped me get up. I was shaking all over. I was so weak and could barely talk. "I...can't...walk" was all that I could say to the man. He was very kind and helped me get to the front row and sit down. My legs were so heavy that I could not cross them. Everyone else was still standing and praising the Lord. Tears were streaming down my face. I knew God was doing a work in me, and I was ready for whatever He had in store for me.

When the songs ended, I thought Chad would come and get me because there was no way I could walk back to my seat.

Chad saw me go down on the floor, but he never saw me get up. He thought that I was down on the floor the entire time. I ended up staying in the front row the whole service. About twenty minutes into the sermon, I started to get my strength back. Later, I found out that the church service was being recorded for a weekly TV program. I was sitting in the front row with all the staff from the church.

When the service ended, I headed back to find Chad. As soon as I saw him, I was overcome with emotion as I retold what I had experienced. I did not grow up with people being "slain in the spirit" and had only seen this on TV. Prior to this, I did not think it was real. Now I was finding out that this was real, and I had been touched with power from the Lord.

Let's look at John 18 when Judas was on his way to betray Jesus. Joining Judas were officers from the chief priest carrying torches and weapons who were intending to arrest Jesus. When Jesus saw them coming, he went forward towards them. The officers asked if he was Jesus and as he said, "I am." They drew backward and fell to the ground. Yes, they were slain in the spirit by Jesus himself. I wonder what kind of power overcame them that day as they fell.

Is every person that goes down on the ground overcome with power? I am not sure. Only that person will truly know. I have had people in ministry push me to try to get me to fall down. I choose to stand with my legs in a stance so that I can "push back" when someone lays hands on me with force. I have even had someone whisper in my ear, "there are two catchers behind you." They wanted me to fall. I want to be overcome with the power of Jesus not put on a show. Wait on Jesus.

When it happens, you will be on the floor and think, "what just happened?"

The same power hit Joshua. He was in Jericho and all the sudden a man appeared in front of him with his sword drawn. Joshua did not know who it was so he said, "Are You for us or for our adversaries" (Joshua 5:13)? The man responded back, "Neither, but as Commander of the army of the Lord I have now come." Joshua fell on his face and worshiped. He was overcome with power and greatness.

As I sought the Lord later about what happened to me, I discovered that "my part" was making better choices in what I was eating. I quit eating foods with wheat or gluten in them. This was a total change from my prior eating habits. Exercise was something that I loved to do. I was going to keep walking. Now I had a walking buddy, Madison, our dog, who loved to walk with me. Our bodies are the temple of God, and if we do not take care of them, who will?

9

ENOUGH IS ENOUGH

I remember having back pain in high school. I was on the dance team and had pain in the evenings after some of the practices. Going to a chiropractor helped some. I tried treatments about once a month to ease the pain. There was not any one thing that I did that caused the pain, so it was hard to predict.

The back pain continued when I went to college. I was on the dance team there as well, and we were known for our high kicks. We practiced four days a week, doing many sets of high kicks at each practice. Shooting pain down the backs of both my legs would come after the long practices. I would head to bed on extreme days and rest.

Back pain was not something that I dealt with every day but when it came, it ruled my life. When my girls were small, if the back pain came, I would push through so I could still pick them up and do the daily chores around the house. Thankfully, I have a wonderful husband who helped out when I was down on my back. Pushing through the pain is something that you get used to when living with chronic pain.

Living on the road required finding a chiropractor to relieve my pain every time we moved. I found that if I went about every six weeks for an adjustment, I would be all right.

Then the pain started coming more often. When it hit, it felt like a knife in my lower back. It would begin when I was doing normal daily things like getting a spoon out of the drawer. SNAP! The pain would take my breath away. I would freeze where I was. I would head to the couch for three to five days with ice on and off my back.

It is hard to be a mom of two girls, a wife, and a homeschool teacher when you are on the couch. There are countless other titles that go along with being a mom like cook, maid, grocery shopper, problem solver, lost things finder, clothes washer, taxi driver and the list goes on and on. In January 2010, down I went. The pain was greater this time than ever before. It was hard to stand, sit, drive, get up, and everything in between. I put a folding chair inside our camper to sit in because it was too hard to get up off the couch. The pain was coming more often than it had in the past and I was down more than ever. I had enough of this pain and being unable to function. The Bible is clear that God has good plans for me, plans for me to prosper, have a future and hope

(Jeremiah 29:11). Chronic back pain was not his will for my life. This was the plan of the enemy to keep me from doing what I was created to do.

I walked into my bedroom and shut the door. Tears began to fall as I cried out to the Lord. I'm 39 and have pain this bad? Really? How will it be when I'm 50? I held my Bible up to the Lord and said, "If this book is real, then I am getting healed." I was not sure that the Bible was real in the area of healing. It had not been proven to me personally. I sat down, opened my Bible, and began to confess the Word out loud. I had no idea how I was going to be healed but I knew that I was going to get it.

The Word of God says that there is power in our speaking (Proverbs 18:21). It also says, "By His stripes we are healed" (Isaiah 53:5). If the Bible is true, then I decided to stand on God's Word UNTIL I received my healing. At this point in my life, I did not know anyone personally that had received full healing from the Lord. I knew many people who were sick and got worse over time. I knew many who got sick and died because of diseases. I only heard some testimonies from the different churches we attended about people who were sick and God healed them. I saw that they were well now. It was mind boggling. I was not sure what I was proposing to the Lord, but I was in desperate need of change.

Each time I had shooting pain in my back, I said, "By the stripes of Jesus, I am healed." I whispered it. No one knew but me that I was confessing the Word over my body. I must have said that verse over 100 times that day but still had the pain. The next day, I got up and thought for sure that I was going to be healed. Then I immediately felt the pain as I scooted out of bed. "By the stripes of Jesus, I am healed," I said quietly so I would not wake my husband. With each step, I kept the faith that Jesus heals. The Bible says, "Jesus is the same yesterday, today, and forever" (Hebrews 13:8). I was trusting The Word.

I decided not to tell anyone about believing for healing and confessing scriptures over my body. In case it did not work, I would not look crazy. It was a secret thing between the Lord and me. I was not 100% sure this would work. The Bible says that it is living, powerful, and sharper than any two-edged sword but I had not seen that yet with healing (Hebrews 4:12).

By lunchtime on the second day, I was completely healed. I felt something lift off me like a coat. I was still careful in my movements as I walked around because never had the pain lifted that quickly. I was shocked that God's Word did the healing when I spoke it out. It was an "ah-ha" moment for me that changed who I was and what I was about to enter into. In that moment, having been in chronic pain for 22 years, I had to convince my mind that my body was healed. I knew what I was feeling...no pain...but my mind told me that there is no way it was gone. Romans 12:2 talks about being transformed by the renewing of your mind. The mind is extremely powerful. It must be transformed to line up with what God is saying about you.

To grow your faith for healing, listen to the Word of God (Romans 10:17). The best way to hear the Word of God is to say it. It does not have to be loud, just loud enough for you to hear it. A whisper is all that is required. Once your faith grows over time, the Word of God will sink down into your heart. Out of the abundance of the heart his mouth speaks (Luke 6:45). Now the Word is ready to come out as you minister healing to yourself and those around you.

Once I realized that I was really healed, I called my mom to share the news. "Mom, I think God healed me," I said, not understanding what was happening. When you have been in pain for a long time, you forget what "normal" feels like. She rejoiced with me. She was attending a conference that weekend where one of the speakers was talking about healing. I asked her to send me some of the information from that weekend. She did and I began to study healing intensely.

10

LET THE HEALINGS BEGIN...

The healing of my back changed the way I thought of scripture. I needed to learn more about how to use the Word of God for change in my life. I knew that things were turning around for our finances because of the Word that had been spoken by us. Could healings happen as well by merely speaking the Word of God out loud? This was too much for my mind to comprehend, and I wanted to learn more.

The information that my mom sent me on healing came in the mail. It was about a Healing School by Joan Hunter. Her parents, Charles and Frances Hunter, were known as "The Happy Hunters" who had a healing ministry. Now Joan Hunter has a healing ministry near Houston, Texas. I asked my mom to buy me a copy of what she was speaking on because I felt strongly that I wanted to learn more about the power to heal. She sent me the CD of her talk that weekend plus all of her books, including her teaching video on how to heal the sick.

I remember sitting in my RV watching these videos and hearing Joan say, "Healing is easy." Just use the name of Jesus, and it comes. I studied her book and the commands for healing of different sicknesses. Up to this point, I had never prayed over anyone for healing other than my children and my husband. I was intrigued as I watched regular people get healed of sicknesses by someone laying hands on them and speaking to the sickness.

Jesus commanded different things in the Bible like the wind, waves, fig tree and a dead person. So why can't we? We can! When you lay hands on people who are sick, tell the sickness to leave in Jesus' name. I was getting so excited while watching these videos. Then it happened. Someone who lived near me in the RV Park had back pain. Scared and nervous, I asked her if it was okay for me to pray for her back to be healed. She approved and I prayed with her. I had enough faith for back pain to be healed. I knew God could heal her. I prayed and she was healed. A week later, her pain came back. I prayed again, and she got healed again. The pain returned again. This was not working out the way I had planned it. I went back a third time and shared how unforgiveness can block healing. I told her to ask the Lord if there was someone that she needed to forgive, and it might even be herself. She asked the Lord, prayed, and the pain finally left for good once she had forgiven.

I heard of another lady in our RV Park that had fallen into a hole and hurt her back. My daughters played with her granddaughter after school and she had mentioned her grandmother's back pain. My confidence was getting a little stronger since I was listening to the teachings, so I made a plan to go to her home and ask to pray for her indoors. I did not want to pray for her in the RV Park because there is not much space between RVs and people are watching you. It is not like they are watching on purpose, but if their blinds are open, they naturally look outside. I did not need or want an audience.

The day I was going to visit her, she stopped by to sell me chocolate bars from her granddaughter's school. I asked her kindly if I could come over later and I would pray with her. She responded, "No, they did that at that church across the street, and it did not work." I was taken back and all I could say was, "Oh, okay." We chatted for a few more minutes and then she said, "Well, if you really want to pray, just go ahead, right here, real quick." Now I was really taken back. This is not how I planned it! I did not have my prayer book, but I started praying anyway, saying any kind of healing prayer that I remembered. The entire time I was praying, she was rolling her eyes and making "sigh" sounds. It was extremely uncomfortable. I was thinking that people were watching as she was making these facial expressions because we were outside in the open. This was not going well. I could not wait to get inside so I prayed as fast as I could. I said, "Amen and goodbye" and raced inside. I got my girls around and told them that she would not get healed; she had no faith, and she acted very rude while I was praying.

Then I went into my small bedroom and closed the door. I

got down on my knees and asked the Lord if there was any way that He could still heal her. I was acting like the man in the story in Mark 9:17-23 when he brought his son to Jesus. His son was demon possessed and needed deliverance and healing. The dad said in Mark 9:22, "But if you can do anything, take pity on us and help us." Then Jesus replies, "If you can? Everything is possible for him who believes." I was trying to believe that the older lady would somehow be healed, but it was hard. Nothing in the natural was causing me to believe that she would receive healing.

One of the names of Jesus is Jehovah Rapha. His name is HEALER. Yes, He can heal, and He wants all people healed. "Beloved, I wish above all things that you be in health and prosper even as your soul prospers" (3 John 1:2). Your soul is made up of three parts: your mind, your will, and your emotions. Jesus wants every single part of you whole and healed.

A few days passed and the granddaughter came over again to play. I asked her how her grandmother was doing. "Fine," she answered. Then I asked how her back was doing, and she stopped dead in her tracks, looked at me with really big eyes, pointed directly at me and said, "My grandma said that you are a healer!" I smiled from ear to ear and said, "Oh, no, it's Jesus! He is the Healer," and my faith grew. I was blown away that she had been healed.

Shortly afterward, I flew to Atlanta to attend a homeschool convention and reunite with some sweet friends I had met while living in Georgia. I was staying with a young lady at the hotel who was also at the conference. As we got ready for bed, she complained of having a terrible headache. I felt the urge to pray for her but did not offer. I did not want my first impression to be "weird" since I just met her.

The next morning we ate breakfast together. We visited and got to know each other a little better. As we were walking out of our room to check out, she complained again about her head hurting. I turned my roller suitcase around and asked her if I could pray for her. She agreed. As soon as I touched her, my hand heated up like a heating pad. It shocked me. I asked her if she felt the heat sensation. She said that as soon as I touched her, her entire body heated up. Wow!

Jesus is the light of the world (John 8:12). When we get close to any light source, we can feel heat. Jesus was reaching down to heal this young lady. We are his hands and feet and when we reach out to heal the sick as Jesus instructed us to do, it is like He is touching them through us.

Shortly after my trip, we were on the road again. This time, we moved to Southaven, Mississippi, to a beautiful RV park. I had no idea what the Lord had in store for me, but I knew He was taking me to a higher level!

11

HAYDEN

As we pulled into the Jellystone RV Park in Southaven, Mississippi, we were pleasantly surprised. This was by far the cleanest RV Park that we had ever seen. It had a nice pool, cabins, a large pavilion, rental bikes, movies for the children and weekly wagon rides with Yogi Bear around the park. We were thankful to be staying at a place that keeps the grass mowed and the trash picked up. It makes a huge difference.

We went to the pool soon after arriving. I noticed specific things about some of the children at the pool. One boy wore special white socks in the pool that I thought was odd. I later found out that he had been in a fire and had severe burns. Another little boy, only six years old, was in a wheelchair. He had a scar on his back that was almost as long as his spinal cord. His dad would tenderly pick him up and sit with him on the edge of the pool so that he could put his feet in the water.

The RV Park was only 20 minutes away from St. Jude Children's Research Hospital in Memphis, Tennessee. St. Jude is totally free for children with severe illnesses. The children that I saw at the pool were staying at the RV Park while getting treatments at the hospital.

A sweet, older man and his wife ran the park. They loved the Lord and we would often talk about Jesus and how He was working in their lives. They gave me all the details on the children in the park so I could pray. The man taught a Bible study one morning each week that was open to all the people staying in the RV Park.

One day in June, as I was driving home, the Lord spoke to me and told me, "Go and pray for the little boy in the wheelchair." I was so shocked that He would want me to pray for him. I had back pain faith, not wheelchair faith. I told the Lord that I would pray about praying for him but would not be visiting him anytime soon. I did, however, find out as much as possible about the little boy.

Hayden was six years old and was from a northern state. He was playing on a T-ball team and his parents noticed that he was complaining about his back hurting. They took him to get an x-ray and found nothing wrong. He went back to playing T-ball, and continued to complain. They decided to take him to get an MRI and what they found changed their lives. He had a cancerous tumor that was wrapped around his entire spinal cord. He was taken immediately to a children's hospital and had surgery in May, one month prior. They thought that he would never walk again. He was able to stand for a short time but was unable to walk; therefore, he used a wheelchair to get around.

A few weeks went by and the Lord nudged me again to go and pray for Hayden. I refused out of fear and ignored the call. It was "way out of my league," and I was not comfortable, so I did nothing. God is so good and was so patient with me. He waited a little longer before calling me again.

It was now July 4, 2010; six months after I was healed of back pain, and the RV Park had a parade. Yogi Bear was leading in his wagon while all the kids in the park rode their bikes, scooters, and golf carts which were decorated with streamers and flags. I noticed that Hayden was there on his electric four-wheeler. He looked like all the other kids when he sat on that four-wheeler. The only difference was when he got stuck on a small incline, he could not move because his feet were stuck in one place. I saw his dad run up beside him to help. Hayden's dad turned him around and helped him get back onto the path, just like our Father in heaven, running to meet us where we are when we need Him.

After the parade, we headed back home to get ready for a cookout. Chad was going to grill outside and I was going to make a few things inside. As I walked into the kitchen, I heard the Lord say, "I said, go pray for Hayden, now!" This time was more stern than the last. So, I went into my bedroom and got on my knees. I asked the Lord one more time, "Do you want me to go and pray for Hayden?" "Go, now," said the Lord. I was scared, but I got my prayer book and walked outside to tell Chad. He said, "Are you sure this is not just you?" I assured him that it was the Lord and that I would be back after a while. I got in my car, drove up to the front of the RV Park where Hayden lived, and I went to the door. As I walked closer to their door, all my fear and anxiety left. I knew God was with me even though I could not see the results yet.

I knocked on the door of the camper and Hayden's dad answered still chewing his July 4th meal. I said, "Hello, my name is Debbie, and the Lord has laid it on my heart to pray for your son." "Well, who is Debbie?" he replied. What a tough question! I was sure my eyes were going to pop out of my head as I pondered, "Who am I?" I was not sure why God had told me to do this. This was not normal to knock on someone's door and ask to pray for them. Why was God talking to me like this? Why me? Many thoughts were racing through my mind but I calmly answered, "I live in the RV Park and was a children's minister." My thought was that if he knew that I liked children and was his neighbor, he would let me pray for his son.

He came outside with me at that point and sat down. We began to talk about Hayden. He told me the entire story. His wife came outside for a while in between taking care of Hayden and the other two children inside. We ended up talking for about an hour. I led him in some prayers breaking off all of the things that could be roadblocks to healing. We did this before Hayden was there. Prayers included: word curses, repentance, generational sins, and unforgiveness. Hayden's dad was open to healing. He was a Christian and knew that God was in the healing business. The week before a man who was a witch doctor from an Indian tribe came to him wanting to pray for Hayden. He did not let him. He made sure all prayers were done in the name of Jesus, the matchless name!

After about an hour of talking and praying, they brought young Hayden outside and sat him in his wheelchair right in front of me. I laid my hand on him and read some prayers for about two minutes. He began to cry because he did not know me. As soon as I was finished, his mom ushered him back inside.

I talked to the dad some more as he was intrigued about healing. I headed home knowing that God had done a huge thing. The next morning, I was up and looking for the family to come and find me. I knew that they were going to tell me some great news. I was not sure what that would be but I knew that something had happened, and they were going to come looking for me.

Nothing happened. All day I waited and never saw them. I was disappointed. I knew God had spoken to me and that I did what God had told me to do. The following day was Wednesday. I woke up early and got on my bike with my Bible under my arm to go to the Bible study under the pavilion. The same sweet couple led it and we prayed at the conclusion. Then we started talking as we always did. The wife said, "Oh, did you hear about Hayden?" "No," I admitted but was eager to hear what happened. "He walked last night," she said. I almost jumped up and hugged her except that my body was in shock. "You mean he took a step or two?" I inquired. "Oh no, he walked the entire length of this pavilion last night," she told me. "Wow, I prayed for him on Monday night and God really did heal him," I mentioned, still not believing what I was hearing.

Sadly, the next day, my girls and I were off to Texas to spend our two weeks visiting family and friends. I did not get to see Hayden before I left and had no idea if he would still be staying there when I returned. To God be all the glory for this miracle. Jesus loves Hayden so much!

As we went to Texas, I asked the Lord who He wanted me to pray for and He gave me three names. Two were old friends that I had not seen or heard from in years. The other was a family member who had been sick for some time.

My girls went to stay with their cousins for one week and I had time alone. The year before, we had built a small home in Texas so we would have a place of our own when we came to visit family. I spent the days seeking the Lord through worship, praying and reading the Word. I contacted those three people and asked if I could come over and pray for them. They let me and all three of the people I prayed with were healed. The fire of God (the heat sensation) was coming more and more when I prayed for people. It was so much fun to pray and watch others receive healing.

I called a friend of mine from high school who had a sick son. I met her on the side of a road and prayed for her son. He did not receive a healing. I was so sad about that. There are roadblocks to healing and, at times, we have to work through those in order to find the root of the illness. Once the root is dealt with, just like with Hayden's dad, healing will come.

Soon our time in Texas was over and we went back to Mississippi in full hope that Hayden would still be around. Sure enough, he was. I waited a few days until I saw his mom outside and then went over to talk with her. She told me that they were seeking the Lord and taking the whole sickness day by day. Then, without warning, Hayden came speeding around the corner on his electric four-wheeler. This time, he parked it, got off and walked. It was one the greatest days of my life. I prayed, God moved, and now Hayden is walking.

God has good plans for each of us. "For I know the thoughts that I think toward you, says the Lord, thoughts of peace and not of evil, to give you a future and a hope" (Jeremiah 29:11). We must be obedient to the ways of God. They are higher than we can imagine. I am so thankful that I was (finally) obedient to the Lord because now Hayden is walking. Praise Jesus!

The Lord laid it on my heart to become ordained in October 2010. So I flew to Magnolia, Texas, to get ordained by Joan Hunter Ministries. She taught me more in the four days of the Healing School than I had learned from her videos. At this point, I was ready to lay hands on and pray for anyone willing.

We were only in Mississippi a short time. My husband had an established business with 15 employees. One employee, Johnny, had some uncomfortable pains in his left side under his ribs. We went out for lunch and after ordering his food, Johnny left the table. The pain was so great, that it hurt him to sit down.

When our food arrived, he came inside. I asked him if I

could pray for him and his response was the most unusual that I had heard. He said, "I do not care if you slap me across the face, just get the pain to stop." He had been in the hospital two times before for a week each and the doctors could not figure out why he had the pain. All he wanted was some relief.

I told him that I would go home and get my Joan Hunter prayer book and come to the office. Once I got home, I did some reading about the cause of side pain and found nothing. So, I spent some time in prayer on my knees. I was getting "prayed up" and ready to be used by God.

By the time I arrived to the office, he had gone home because the pain was so strong. I was disappointed. I inquired of the Lord about this and gently he responded to me saying, "What I have given you is a gift and I am always ready for you to use it." What I learned that day is that we are the hands and feet of Jesus. We each have gifts and when there is a person in front of us that needs a touch from the Lord, we must be ready at all times. It does not matter how much of the Bible we have read that day or even if we prayed. Hear me on this, it is good to read your Bible and good to pray but if you wake up late one day and do not have time to do those things, God can still use you.

The next morning, I went early to the office. Johnny was there. My husband and I went into the office with him and shut the door. I commanded the pain to leave in Jesus' name and the fire of God showed up. Both Johnny and I felt our bodies fill up with heat. God is light. When you get close to a light bulb, you feel the heat. Jesus is the same way. When he comes down to heal and touch you, at times, there will be a heat sensation.

Johnny's eyes got large as he felt the heat move through his body and all the pain vanish. He was in awe. I asked him if he had ever received Jesus as Lord and Savior and he had not. That day, he got saved and healed.

When we ask Jesus into our hearts, we have everything that He has. Holy Spirit wants to come and live inside of us. Prayer and reading the Bible daily will help you in your walk as well as fasting and attending church. But when the time comes to encourage someone, pray for healing, or help someone out, that is not the time to go and lock yourself in your prayer closet. Be ready to be used by God. We are his hands and feet on the earth today. He uses us and commands us to "Go!" just like He told the disciples. "Heal the sick, raise the dead, cleanse those who have leprosy and drive out demons" (Matthew 10:8).

It was time, once again, to hit the road. The night before we left, I had a dream. In the dream, I was sitting in a courtyard with my doctor from Texas. He asked me where I was living now. I told Him that tomorrow I was moving to Arizona. He asked me what I was going to do there. I told him that I was going to have a camp there for children.

For years, Chad and I had talked about having a Christian summer camp for kids and youth. At times, while living on the road, we would get a map out, spread it on the table and study it. We would ask each other, "Where do you want to live and why?" It was always somewhere in the South with water, rolling hills and trees. Arizona was never an option because there are no trees, little water, and no grass but there is a lot of cactus for children to fall into.

I told Chad about my dream, and he was not excited. He blew it off and said, "We are only going to work in Arizona for a few months." But I knew that the doctor in my dream represented Jesus, The Great Physician, and if Jesus and I had that conversation, then it would happen. Many dreams I forget by the time I brush my teeth in the morning, but not this one. I still remember every single word and am hopeful to have a camp in Arizona one day.

12

THE NINTH AND FINAL STATE

As I went about my normal life, the Lord started speaking to me more and more when I was out in public. He would tell me to pray for certain people. It was so scary. Most of the time I obeyed. I would say, "Hey, what is going on with your leg?" Surprisingly, strangers would tell me what was happening. I then asked them if I could pray and a majority of them would say "yes," bow their head, and close their eyes. It was shocking at first because I had to leave my eyes open to watch what was happening around us. It was fun to see the reactions of other people trying to figure out what I was doing. My family was adjusting to me praying for strangers. It was all completely new. We did not know anyone at the time doing this.

The trip to Arizona was long. We stopped along the way to break up the trip, but anytime you are traveling with an RV, the trip is longer. We visited White Sands, New Mexico, and rented some sleds to slide down the sand dunes. What a great day we had playing in the sand! We experienced two flat tires on the RV, which made for an extended time of travel.

Once in Phoenix, the beauty of the desert captivated us. It was not the same as the South. Rugged mountains surround the city and grass is sparse, but it is clean and the sun is out almost every day. The pool was heated at the RV Park and we spent many days swimming in an outdoor pool in November and December. That was different for us. My children enjoyed it!

We quickly found a church and it had Healing Rooms. I was excited to help out and learn from others while laying hands on the sick. When I called for information, the man informed me that I had missed the training by two weeks, and they would not be having another training session until next year. With our record of moving, I was unsure whether or not we would still be around. I was upset with God. I took this to prayer, and He said, "I did not call you to the church." What? Why not? The church is easy. The people come to you for healing. I did not want to be "called" to Wal-Mart, Hobby Lobby, Famous Footwear, and other stores. I know there are sick people there, but it is a stretch to ask a complete stranger if they want prayer.

So, it is. God called me to people in places other than the church. I was upset for a while and did not pray for anyone when I was out. I knew there were certain people that I was to pray for, but I was in rebellion against healing for a time. That only lasted a few weeks and I started praying for strangers again. I would look for people who were limping, had a brace or openly shared their sickness with me. That was my cue to offer to pray.

One day in January 2011, I had fixed my children breakfast and was cleaning up the kitchen while listening to them talk. One of them was complaining because she had no friends while the other was complaining that she wanted her own room. I began to cry. I could not hold back the tears. We had been living on the road for five years. Arizona was the ninth state we had moved to. We had not always been in the RV; but the majority of the time we were, and it was getting tight. I turned around with tears streaming down my cheeks and started telling my girls, "I am sorry. I am sorry that we do not have any friends. I am sorry that we live in this RV and have limited room. I am sorry that you do not have your own room. I am sorry that we have to homeschool." We were all tired of this lifestyle. I exited to my room and hit my knees. It was there that I began a deep sob from my inner most being. "When, God, when?" I begin to plead and "Why, God, why?" My heart hurt for my family, as we seemed to be stuck in this lifestyle. I was ready for a change. Little did I know that change was so close that I could have reached out and grabbed it.

Chad had never been in favor of staying in Arizona. We heard about the heat and he did not want to still be there in the summer even though we are from Texas and used to the heat. Chad was also antsy from living in the RV. He is an entrepreneur and always had a project to work on or experiment with. It had been a long time since he was able to do that due to the fact we had no room or garage for him to create in.

About a week after I cried out to God, Chad woke me up at 6:00 am and told me of a new invention he had. He was going to rent a space to work out of that was close to the RV Park. I was ok with that. So that day he began to look for an office with a warehouse to rent. The very next morning, he woke me up again at 6:00 am with a new idea. "How about we rent a house and I can work out of the garage?" I leaped up! "Did you say rent a house?" I repeated back, still half asleep. I would waste no time looking up houses for rent that day.

Only God could orchestrate us finding a house the next day and moving the next week. The kids were so excited that they loaded the car with all their toys days before we actually moved in. We had no furniture except the couch from our RV and some chairs. We did not mind one bit.

The house had three bedrooms so Holly and Heidi had their own rooms. We had a pool in the back along with a hot tub, outdoor kitchen, and a waterfall in the front and back yards. God is good! It was like we moved into a resort.

Holly and Chad flew to Alabama to load up our belongings that had been in storage for three years. They hauled our things all the way to Arizona, a three-day drive. It was like Christmas when we opened each box. We did not remember what we had packed so many years ago.

Our situation was quickly changing. It did not stop there.

One week later, my children started going to a Christian school a few miles from our house. "Wow, God!" In only a few days, I went from teaching school in an RV to living in a nice house with my children in school. What a change! It is coming, but we must keep the faith and be patient. No matter the season, we must keep the faith and trust the Lord because change is coming.

Two years later we bought a house in Phoenix while our children were still attending Christian school. Once we realized that we were staying in Arizona, we began to look for a youth camp. We found one that we believe one day we will own. We are waiting on the Lord for the right timing.

The Lord taught me about healing and now wanted me to teach others. In January 2012, I taught a healing class in my home for the first time. It was called Healing Hands and there were 20 people that attended. The goal was to teach others how to lay hands on the sick and watch God heal them. We had healings and miracles happen in the class from the very beginning. It was great! I am still receiving reports from those in the class and the healings that they are experiencing. It is having a snowball effect. As those in the class are seeking more of Jesus, He is opening doors for them to lay hands on the sick and minister healing. God's purpose for me now is not to pray for as many people as I can, but to teach others how simple it is to pray for the sick and watch them recover. Open up your heart, believe, and learn how to pray for the sick. You can do it. It is easy! Only believe!

13

VOICE ACTIVATED

Christianity can be called *The Great Confession.* Most Christians that are defeated in life are defeated because they believe and confess the wrong things. They have spoken the words of the enemy and WORDS will hold you in bondage. The Bible is clear about the power of the spoken word. It states "You are ensnared by the words of your mouth; You are taken by the words of your mouth" (Proverbs 6:2).

The Word of God is powerful! It is very important to understand this truth and act on it. Many do not know what to do or how to activate it. Let's get moving in the things of God. James 1:22 says, "Be doers of the word, and not hearers only, deceiving yourselves." "You will also declare a thing and it will be established for you" (Job 22:28).

Words are containers. They carry faith or fear and they produce after their kind. We must speak God's Word out loud in order to be effective. Creative power will come forth from words spoken in faith. The Word of God is only powerless when it is NOT spoken. When God created the entire world, He spoke. Just mere words created this universe.

We must repent for words not spoken in faith. Complaining, griping, gossiping, and the like MUST stop. Pause for a moment and repent for words that you have spoken over others. Jesus wants us to encourage one another, lift others up, and be a blessing to everyone that we come in contact with each day (Romans 14:19, Hebrews 10:25).

The Word of God is living and powerful, and sharper than any two-edged sword (Hebrews 4:12). When we speak, things happen! The angels excel in strength and do His word, heeding the voice of His word (Psalm 103:20). They are waiting until someone speaks the Word so they can go to work. Are you giving them some work to do or the day off?

A few years ago, while we were homeschooling, we did an experiment that we heard about and thought that it would be fun. We took regular brown rice and cooked it. Then we placed it in two separate plastic containers, labeled them, and left them on the counter out of the sun. One was labeled "The Good Rice" and the other was "The Bad Rice." On the good rice, we placed stickers and the bad rice received no stickers. Then, we did something quite strange; we began to talk to the rice.

The Bible says that there is "the power of life and death in the tongue" (Proverbs 18:21). We wanted to find out if rice that was identical in the beginning responded differently to positive and negative words. We began to pick up the good rice and say in a sweet voice "You are so kind. You are good. You look nice." But to the bad rice, we spoke in a really mean tone and said things like "You stink. You will die. You are ugly. I do not like you." After only one day, the good rice looked exactly the same, but the bad rice had swollen up and looked like the lid was going to pop off. We were shocked.

We got to where we did not speak to the rice every day, but we labeled it and that still had an effect. Isn't that just like us? Don't we refer to people according to their sicknesses? "Oh, that is the man with the cane," or "The lady that has cancer lives there" or maybe "The child that is out of control is in that class." Do we not know how much effect our words have on others?

After a while, the good rice changed a little bit, looking like uncooked rice. The bad rice did not look the same. It grew a layer of white mold on the top. We kept the rice for about a year and never did the good rice grow mold. Words are containers. There is power in your mouth.

What are you saying about your body? "I will probably get the stomach bug because we always pass it around our family when one person gets it." Stop confessing those words of death. Choose life (Deuteronomy 30:19). "My leg is killing me." Really? Your leg is killing you? "I am so stupid." No, you are not. The Bible says, "We have the mind of Christ" (1 Corinthians 2:16) and "God created man in His own image" (Genesis 1:27). Change your words and you will change your thoughts, your life, and your destiny.

The centurion asked Jesus to speak a "word" and a boy would be healed. Jesus said to the centurion, "Go! It will be done just as you believed it would" (Matthew 8:13). The little boy was restored to health at that very moment.

The centurion had a positive, believing attitude and Jesus did what was asked of him. Positive minds produce positive lives. Thoughts that are positive contain faith. Negative minds produce negative lives, which are full of fear and unbelief. "For as a man thinks in his heart, so is he" (Proverbs 23:7). What do you spend your time thinking on?

For over a year, I had this burning sensation on my tongue. After much research, I discovered it was called "Burning Tongue Syndrome." I had the opportunity for a lady who has a healing ministry to pray for me. I described to her what was happening, I said, "My tongue hurts so bad. It is killing me!" She looked me right in the eye and said, "Do not say that again." Then she prayed for me. We must be careful what we are confessing over our bodies.

I had experience with laying hands on the sick and seeing healings and miracles in person. However, one day I received an out-of-state phone call. A lady in her 60's had major surgery where she was opened in the front and back of her body for stomach issues and back problems. She was in the recovery room after having additional problems when they put me on speakerphone. Another lady in the room put her hands on her. I prayed aloud, and shortly thereafter her doctor reported that she was now recovering like a 30-year-old. We have authority in the spiritual realm so our words cannot be contained by time and space. It did not matter that we were three states apart; healing came when the Word of God was spoken. Praise Jesus! He is so awesome!

"Faith comes by hearing, and hearing by the word of God" (Romans 10:17). When we hear God's Word spoken, we are gaining faith. However, when we begin to put that faith in motion and speak it out, it becomes activated in our lives. Daily declarations of the Word of God are one key to daily victory.

14

SET FREE

While Jesus was on the earth, he walked in miracles and healings with signs and wonders following him everywhere that he went. Mark 9:14-29, mentions a man who had a son that was demon possessed. He brought his son to Jesus and asked him, "If you can do anything, have compassion on us and help us?" Jesus was taken back and said, "If you can believe, all things are possible?" Of course Jesus can help him. Jesus responded with this simple question, "Can you believe?" All Jesus needs is someone to believe that He is who He says He is and that He can do what we think is impossible.

From this passage, I understand that deliverance from demons and healings are related. First, Jesus cast off the spirit, and then healing came to the boy. I have searched high and low and have a hard time finding Bible-based teachings on the demonic these days. Why is this? Why has the church pushed the demonic aside when some healings are directly related to the demonic? When was the last time you heard of a pastor casting out a demon or preaching on the demonic realm?

Right before Jesus ascended into heaven, he gave these last instructions to his closest friends, the disciples. "Heal the sick, cleanse the lepers, raise the dead, and cast out demons" (Matthew 10:8). Those are some tall orders that we are to fill. How are we able to do these things? Where do we start? Those same commands are for us today. We are supposed to be doing the works that Jesus did and even greater (John 14:12).

These were questions that boggled my mind. Where do I learn how to do this? What steps do I take to help others get free from demonic oppression in their lives?

In the fall of 2011, I went to a healing and deliverance training at my church because I wanted answers. In the class, we watched a training video of a man speaking. My questions were not fully answered. At the end of the class, I began to talk to those in the room that had the same desire I did. It was then that a man gave me a business card and told me to go check out The House of Healing in Phoenix, Arizona, because they did group deliverance. I was interested and wanted to go. I asked a friend if she would go with me, and we went a few weeks later.

I am so thankful for friends who are willing to go with me to certain places because this is one place I did not want to go alone. It was located in an office building off a main street in downtown Phoenix. It was dark when we arrived. I quickly scanned the entire room once we entered. A peculiar bunch of people filled the room waiting for the speaker to start. There were about 45 people who seemed to have an addicted to drugs or alcohol. We sat near the back because I wanted to take in as much as possible.

The main speaker, Mike, began to talk; I was shocked. He spoke about demons, healings and miracles in a way I had never heard. He taught for two hours on the unseen, spiritual world. I took many notes and sat there in awe. This is the kind of teaching that I had been searching for. When his speaking time ended, he took a break before beginning the group deliverance.

I found a "normal looking" woman that worked there and asked her what to expect during the deliverance time. I wanted to be prepared as my friend and I were unsure of what was about to happen. She told me that there would be some scriptures read and then the demons would be commanded to come out. They will come out; possibly with some manifestations like animal sounds or shrieking.

What? I had never experienced anything like this. This was going to be interesting. We took our seats and were ready to watch. The scriptures were spoken and the demons were commanded to come out. In the next few moments, my mind was blown away at what was happening. Just like in the Bible when Jesus commanded the evil spirits to come out, we witnessed shrieking and violent convulsions as the demons were cast out (Mark 9:26). I saw all of this and more. It was overwhelming. People were coughing, sneezing, throwing up, and some were on the floor getting delivered.

I felt the urge to cough but was holding it in. I could see that the people working the room were walking around praying for people. The workers all had badges. I could tell that they had authority and used it in the spirit realm. Mike started to walk toward me and I was not sure what was about to take place. He came up to me, grabbed my hands, rubbed the palms of his hands on mine saying, "I anoint you with everything that I have. Now go and do what God has called you to do." I was in shock at this point. I began to pray to the Lord and forgot all the activity happening around me. I wanted to obey God and help all those that are in my life.

My friend and I left shortly after that. We went out to the car and began to belly laugh really hard like a bunch of schoolgirls. We both were coughing non-stop as we rehearsed the events of the night. What an experience! We were both in agreement not to go back to that place and were unsure if we would share our experience. It was so far "out there." Not many people would believe us.

Somehow I ended up on The House of Healing's email list and received their updates on healings, miracles, and classes to come. A different friend had been struggling with an illness for some time and when I mentioned going to The House of Healing, she was all for it. They were having a special time for women only. That would be better due to all the scary people that were there the last time. We planned to meet and go in together.

This time, every seat was taken except in the front row. It had been only a few months since I last attended and the news had spread of what Jesus was doing in the lives of many hungry people looking for freedom from sickness and disease. My friend led me to the front row, center section. We sat through the two-hour teaching and stayed for the group deliverance.

This time was a different. They called women to come forward if they had sickness in their body. About 10 came to the front, and then Mike started commanding the demonic strongholds to break and for healing to come. I was sitting with my elbows on my knees bent over praying for my friend. Mike came by and placed his hand on my back as he prayed for me. I let out a scream that even scared me! He passed and I decided that since I was a little spooked, I would keep my eyes open.

A few moments later, he passed again and this time he placed his hand on my head. I jumped and got a chill from one end of my body to the other. He grabbed my hand and pulled me to the front with him. He said, "You have a spirit of fear. Where did it come from?" I said, "I do not know." "Yes, you do," he continued, "now tell me where it came from."

The truth is, I did know when it came on me. About 20 years ago, while in college, I was stalked by a man. He came into where I worked and charmed me. He asked me out on a date and I met him at an end-of-the-year party. He took me home and from there, it got weird. He did not hurt me physically, but mentally he messed with me. He did some strange things that resulted in me contacting the university and city police. Fear entered. I gave Satan a foothold. The demon of fear came right on into my life. Fear had been with me ever since, for nineteen years.

There were times in my life when I had panic attacks. For a season in my life, I would search every closet upon arriving in my home thinking that a man was hiding and waiting to attack me. Fear puts thoughts in your mind and causes you to act strangely. That does not come from God but bondage from the enemy. "God has not given us a spirit of fear, but of power and of love and of a sound mind" (2 Timothy 1:7).

Today, fear was leaving, but I did not yet know how that was going to take place. I finally told Mike that I was stalked and that is when fear entered. He asked me the stalker's name. I honestly could not remember his name. I had blocked it from my memory. Mike cupped his hands and placed them on my stomach and back. He commanded the spirit of fear to come out. I was taking deep breaths over and over. He stopped and I felt a tingling in my stomach. He continued. It moved into my arms. My arms were moving all around almost uncontrollably. I stopped them from moving and I told him that I was sure the spirit of fear was gone. "How will you know?" he asked me. I told him that I was scared of his parking lot and if I could walk outside and not be afraid, then I would be sure it was gone. He said, "Do me a favor and walk outside in the parking lot and then come back in." I was sure that it was gone so I headed for the door.

I took about ten steps outside in the dark when I saw a man. He asked, "How are you doing this evening?" At that moment, I felt something pinch me all along my shoulders. It sent a chill down my entire body. I turned around so fast with tears running down my face. I knew the stronghold of fear was still there. I ran in to where Mike was. "It is still here. I felt it, and it's not gone. HELP ME!"

Mike said, "Forgive your stalker." What happened in the next few minutes is really hard to describe. I was not speaking. The demonic spirit of fear held my tongue. He spoke for me. I yelled, "I don't want to forgive him." Now, in my mind, I was thinking, "I will forgive him," but at that moment, I was not in control. "That is it!" yelled Mike. Due to the fact that I had never forgiven the stalker, the spirit of fear had a right to be there. Mike kept telling me to forgive him and bless him, but I could not. My tongue was being held. Then my mind went into total confusion and I could not remember what to say. I finally said, "Tell me what to say and I will repeat you." So Mike said, "Say, I forgive him." I said, "I...Forgive...Him...I...Bless...Him." Once these words came out, I fell to the ground. All my energy was drained. I began to forgive him for each and every action that he did towards me. Tears were streaming. I had been in a battle with an unclean spirit, and I won. I was exhausted. It took some time but I finally got up off the floor.

I held my head high and went back outside. I walked down to the end of the corner and across the street. I walked around cars and had no fear. I had the victory! I had a demon on me for years and now, it was gone. Praise the Lord! Only Jesus could have done that for me.

Since then, I have gone back many times to the House of Healing. I have taken numerous adults and children. I want all to be free. No one should have to be entrapped like I was with fear for so many years. To God be all the glory for what He has done in my life.

The night after I was freed, I went to a benefit dinner. For the past two years, I followed a gluten-free diet. Gluten affected me in more than one way but the main thing was fatigue. That night at the dinner, the menu was like a wheat feast. Everything offered was full of wheat and gluten. I decided to eat it and pay later for what I ate. That night after dinner, there were no side effects. Not one. Could it be that the spirit of fear and negative effects from gluten are related? I have no medical science to prove this but it worked for me. My daughters, who also ate a gluten-free diet, went the following week to the House of Healing for the children's deliverance service and they both got freed. Today we all eat gluten-filled foods. The best part is the spirit of fear that consumed them is gone.

Once your body is cleaned from the demonic, the Bible is very clear to immediately fill it up with good things like prayer, Bible reading, praising the Lord through songs, and attending church where the Word of God is preached. If it is not consistently filled up with the right things, the enemy will come back and bring seven friends. The Bible tells how the person will be worse off than before (Matthew 12:45).

Jesus said that you will do what he did and even greater (John 14:12). Let's step into the EVEN GREATER part. I am ready! Are you? Just believe...

15

ARE YOU SURE?

The Bible is clear that Jesus is THE WAY. In John 14:6, Jesus states, "I am the way, the truth and the life. No one comes to the Father except through me." You must accept Jesus into your life to be your Lord and Savior to enter into heaven at the end of this lifetime. Ask God to forgive you of your sins. People are going to do mean and hurtful things to us but we cannot hold onto the past. God says forgive. As you ask God to come into your life, your name will be written in the Lamb's book of life (Revelation 21:27). One day, when you enter into heaven, you will see your name written in it. No one can enter unless his or her name is on the list. Reservations are being taken now for the most glorious place in the world. Don't miss out!

If you want to know for sure that you will be in heaven, all that is required is a prayer. The words are not magical for God looks at the heart. Say this prayer out loud.

Prayer for Salvation

Heavenly Father, I come to you in the name of Jesus. You said in your Word that whoever calls on the name of the Lord shall be saved. Father, I am calling on Jesus right now. I believe He died on the cross for my sins, that he was raised from the dead on the third day, and He is alive right now.

Lord Jesus, I am asking You to come into my heart and be the Lord of my life. I repent of my sins and surrender myself completely to You. I declare that Jesus is Lord over my life. Amen (Romans 10:9, 13).

Once you have said this prayer, your name is entered into the Lamb's book of life (Revelation 13:8). Your name will be checked upon arrival into heaven. Please note that your name will be spelled correctly because Jesus knows everything about you. Congratulations are in order! Heaven rejoices when one sinner repents and decides to follow Jesus (Luke 15:10). Now step into this new lifestyle believing the words Jesus spoke that are true and still alive today.

16

HEALING ENCOUNTERS

The Word confirms in Revelation 12:11 that we overcome by the blood of the Lamb and by the word of our testimony. May each testimony encourage you to step closer to praying for the sick. It is easy. You can do this. Become willing and available and God will use you in a mighty way.

The majority of people I pray for, I only see one time. Often I pray for people in stores like Wal-Mart, Macy's or Home Depot. I do not intentionally search out people to pray for when I go into a store. I do the normal shopping that I need to do for that day while having my eyes open for the sick. The Lord brings people to me. I start talking to them casually; soon we are on the subject of their sickness. That is my cue to ask them if I can pray for them. The majority of the time they say "yes," and then they bow their head and close their eyes. Rule number one, keep your eyes open when you pray for others. I pray exactly what they need. All prayers are done "in the name of Jesus," and I keep the prayer as short as possible. We smile, they thank me and we depart many times not even exchanging names. The only name they need to remember is "Jesus" anyway. In heaven, I will find out all the details of their healing.

Mark 16:18 says "They will lay hands on the sick, and they will recover." The word *recover* in this phrase means "get better over time." So, when you pray for others, believe that they will be healed, but it may not happen right before your eyes. That is where you start walking by faith. Faith is not seen. Hebrews 11:1 says, "Faith is the substance of things hoped for, the evidence of things not seen." You trust Jesus from that point forward. Enjoy these stories and prepare for your own "Healing Encounters."

The lady in beanie hat

I was at a scrapbook retreat. I enjoy scrapbooking and was staying at a Christian campground in the mountains for three nights. The first night our group of ladies went to the chow hall to eat. There was a little old lady with a cane wearing a beanie hat. She looked like a ball of energy. She asked to sit at our table because she had back surgery recently and could not use the steps up to where her group was eating dinner. She sat across the table from me. As she sat down, the Lord whispered to me, "Pray for her." I knew the prayer would come later. After dinner, she scooted out and I was not able to pray with her, but I knew the Lord would give me another chance.

All weekend I looked for her but never saw her again in the chow hall. On the last day, I decided to take a walk. There had been a snowstorm the day before and everything was covered in a thick, white blanket of snow. There was a creek that I wanted to visit and have some time alone with the Lord. I had my gloves on, my iPod, my hoodie, my boots, my warmest clothes and I was on my way when I saw the lady in the beanie. She was in the parking lot packing up her truck. I went up to her and said, "Hello, are you the one who had back surgery." She nodded and we talked for a minute. I asked if I could pray for her and she agreed. I prayed and when I was finished, she smiled and shook her head as she walked around me towards the truck. I thought that was strange so I asked her if she was all right. She said that pain left suddenly and she felt like she was going to pass out. She needed to sit down in the truck. At times, the Lord will touch someone so strongly that they will feel light-headed like they just had a massage. I assisted her in getting into the truck to rest.

There were other women nearby packing their cars. The lady in the beanie was the ringleader and as soon as I began to pray for her, her friends came in close to listen. When I had helped her sit down in the truck, she began to use her cane to point out others that needed healing. The next lady moved forward for prayer. She had something wrong with her foot. I bent down to touch her foot and pray. About halfway through the prayer I stopped and asked her if she was okay. She smiled and said, "I think I am going to pass out." Oh my, the Lord was showing up right here in the parking lot full of snow.

I was standing on her left side with my hands on her arm

and her back. I knew if she moved her feet, she would fall. I called for someone to bring me a chair. Out of nowhere someone opened up a camping chair and we helped her sit back in the chair. When she sat down, her head flew back like a newborn baby's head with no support. By now, the lady with the beanie was by my side. She looked at me and said, "Who are you and where are you from?" (That is my favorite question by the way.) We are not of this world; we are visiting here, walking like Jesus.

I explained that I was at a scrapbook retreat and prayed for people everywhere I go. She was shocked that I was not with a church group at a retreat like she was. She put my name and number in her flip phone.

At this point, I was calm but not sure what was happening. The next person was a sister of the lady with the beanie. She had a rotator cuff problem and could not put her right arm in certain positions behind her back. I put my hands on her shoulder and commanded it to be healed in the name of Jesus. She screamed and then moved her arm in all directions. I thought she was in pain but she was screaming joyfully; without pain she was moving her arm in all directions. The look on her face was priceless. I turned around and calmly said, "Who is next?" The lady with the beanie had told others what was happening and a small crowd had gathered. One lady just wanted to hug me. Another asked me to pray for her son in the military. I made myself available to pray for whoever wanted prayer.

When I was done, I walked to the creek and thanked Jesus for helping me. Without his name, I can do nothing. He is the

Healer, Jehovah-Rapha is His Name. I sure am glad that I decided to take a walk that day in the snow. You never know when God will use you. Become available in your everyday life and watch what happens.

Macy's makeup counter

I entered Macy's department store to buy makeup. I noticed that the sweet lady helping me had a brace on her wrist, which usually means carpal tunnel. We talked about makeup and I asked if she had carpal tunnel. She said, "yes" stating that she had it for so long that now she was having shoulder pain and required physical therapy twice a week. I asked if I could pray for her. She jumped backward placing her hand on her heart and said, "I am Buddhist." "It does not matter what you are, do you want to be healed?" I responded. She was so taken back; she did not know how to answer. She saw some ladies at the other end of the counter and said that she needed to help them and walked away. I was unsure what to do at that point so I waited. The ladies were just looking and motioned for her to return to me. I looked at her and smiled. "Do you want me to pray or not? I need a yes or no?" I finally said. She looked down and said, "I cannot." I smiled and wished her well.

There will be those who do not want to be healed for different reasons. Some might be on disability or get attention from their sickness maybe with a wheelchair or cane. That was a hard one for me to grasp, but I only pray for those who want to be healed. Many times, the person who is sick does not want prayer but their mom or another family member wants you to pray for them. I tell them that all I need is a "yes" from the person and then I will pray.

Our (almost) new neighbors

We were looking to buy a new house and found one we were interested in buying. We met the neighbors and had them over before we bought the house because we liked them and wanted to get to know them better. After dinner, the man mentioned that he had hurt his right shoulder while moving something heavy. I asked him if I could pray and he agreed. He did not know anyone who had ever gotten healed before. I prayed really fast asking God to touch his back. The fire of God came and my hand heated up. He felt the heat all over his shoulder and down his back. Instantly, he was healed. That was several years ago and he still has no pain. We never ended up buying that house but keep in touch.

Itchy rash

A friend called me one night from the Minute Clinic. She had an itchy rash show up that day and it was painful. Usually, not every time, an itchy rash can be related to an offense. I asked her if someone offended her. She thought for a moment and then told me she and her husband had a huge fight that morning and she got offended. I prayed for her on the phone but instructed her to repent and forgive him once we hung up. She did and the itchy rash left that night.

At times, sicknesses will have roadblocks. Once you clear the blockage, healing comes quickly. As you walk with the Lord hand in hand doing healings, Holy Spirit will speak to you about these roadblocks. Every person is different. There are no formulas. There is not an easy four-step technique to follow. Learn to follow Holy Spirit. Ask Him to teach you. He is the helper and teacher (John 14:26).

Some of the common roadblocks are unforgiveness, unrepentance, ungodly soul ties and word curses. Each of these can be taken care of by a simple prayer. Jesus makes everything that we need easy and available. He said to become as little children and He will help you (Matthew 18:3).

My daughter's ear

We were on vacation staying up in the mountains. We spent the night and were getting ready for our day when my daughter, who was nine at the time, began to scream that her ear was hurting. I began to pray but nothing seemed to be working as fast as we wanted. I sent my husband to the store to get some oil so I could put it in her ear. Knowing that he would be gone a while, we started watching Sid Roth: It's Supernatural. In this show, Sid interviews people who have supernatural encounters with the Lord. I was trying to get her mind off the fact that her ear was hurting. As we watched, she began to calm down a little but was still pulling at her ear. I kept praying.

The Word of God says to, "Ask, and it will be given to you; seek and you will find; knock, and it will be opened to you" (Matthew 7:7). Praying is what I have done for years in place of going to the doctor. Being that we moved so much in the RV, we did not have time to find a good doctor in each town we lived in. We prayed and trusted Jesus when we got sick.

My husband finally returned from the store with some olive oil. My daughter looked at him and said, "All the pain is gone, Daddy. God healed my ear." We used the oil for cooking. Thank you, Jesus. He is Faithful and True (Revelation 19:11).

Both of my children have prayed for others while at school. They have grown up watching me pray for people and think it is normal. What if we all did this? What if there was no sickness left in believers? How could we better show the world that Jesus is our healer? Would they believe once they were healed?

DSW shoe store

It was the Saturday before Easter in the shoe store. People were packed in. I was shopping with my daughter who already found shoes so she went to sit down and enjoy a treat while I continued to shop. I found some shoes but a lady was standing in front of them, so I waited. She finally saw me and moved. I noticed that she had the carpel tunnel brace on so I asked her if she wanted me to pray. She looked at me in disbelief and said, "I have been asking the Lord to send someone to pray for me!" This sweet lady had a really loud voice. You know the people who cannot talk quietly if they try. She was super excited and more than ready for me to pray. I prayed out loud quietly, remembering that I am in a shoe store where the counters are low so everyone can see everything.

When I said, "Amen," I thought I was finished but she grabbed my hand and said, "Hold on." Then she turned to an elderly lady near us and said, "Ethel, she is a Christian healer!"

Ethel was her neighbor who she had taken shopping for a new Easter dress and new shoes to wear to church on Sunday. Ethel made her way over to me, backed up and said, "Pray for my hip." I asked her if she fell or hurt it and she replied, "No, just pray, it hurts." They both assumed the prayer position; eyes closed, head bowed but I know rule number one, which is keep your eyes open. Good thing I did because I was the only one who saw the store clerk come up behind me and place her hands on her hips. I was thinking that this was not good. I decided to keep praying and act like I did not see her there.

When we got done the clerk said, "Is everything alright here?" The lady with the loud voice pointing to me and said, "Yes, she is a Christian healer!" She looked at me; I smiled and told her we were fine. I grabbed my shoes and said my goodbyes as I hurried off to the checkout counter before security was called.

Hot air balloon trip

It was Good Friday and my family took a hot air balloon trip over Arizona. There were 15 people in the basket, each in their own "section" of the balloon for weight and balance. In my section was my daughter and I but near us was a mom, a grandma and two small children. When you are that close to others, you tend to "get to know them" especially while experiencing something so awesome as a hot air balloon ride.

It was a fantastic experience until the landing. It was rough. We hit the ground, flipped over backwards and slid. Our "pilot" was stressed and it showed in his actions. The grandma behind me said, "Oh, I think I hurt my back." I looked at her and said, "I have a healing ministry and will pray for your back once we are on the ground." "Oh, I thought you were a Christian," she replied. Once our feet were on the ground, she did not want me to pray for her but got my phone number "just in case." We enjoyed breakfast together in the desert, as it is a hot air balloon tradition and parted ways.

One year later, I received a phone call. "Debbie, you might not remember me but I was on the hot air balloon ride with you." I remembered. She had hurt her back and had been to several doctors and was still in pain. She told me that she lived in a different state and owned a house in Arizona where she currently was. I offered to come to her house to pray the next day.

Her house was fancy. We met in the "guest suite" which was beautiful. She kept mentioning that her husband was well known but I did not know his name or what he did. We had a wonderful session of prayer. She opened up and told me her story that not many people knew.

Once we were finished, she gave me a tour of her home and I met her husband, still not recognizing his name or his face. Once I got home, I did a little research and found out that he was the owner of an NFL football team.

I asked the Lord why he would take me to their home to minister. He told me that both rich and poor need healing. The rich, at times, are the hardest to reach because of their status. The sweet lady and I are still friends today. We stay in contact several times a year.

Office Max

I was standing at the counter at Office Max getting some ministry things copied when I met Tim. He was a mechanic who was sent to Office Max because the printer stopped working at his office. He walked up and we began to talk. He looked at the copies where my picture was and asked, "Is that you?" "Yes, I have a healing ministry. Do you have any sickness in your body?" That question totally caught him off guard and he replied, "Oh, where would I start?" He laughed and walked away.

If we look at Jesus in the Bible, he prayed for those who came to him. He did not beg people to receive prayer nor did he chase people down to pray with them. I do the same. I offer healing and then wait for a response. At times, people will want prayer and other times they think I am weird. I am good either way. My job is to offer to pray.

In this case, Tim paid for his items then returned to me and said, "What do you do again?" I told him that I pray for people that are sick and asked if he had any pain in his body. This time, he said that his right elbow hurt. I touched his wrist because many times, the "tunnel" under the skin is pressed down and the blood cannot flow from the wrist to the elbow. (This is also the problem with carpal tunnel.) I commanded the tunnel to open, the blood to flow, and all the pain to leave in the name of Jesus. The prayer was fast and quiet as I was standing at the copy counter in Office Max.

Then I told Tim to check his elbow. He screamed, "Whoa!" "What is happening?" I asked. He said that all the pain was gone. Then he looked at me real seriously and said, "Does Jesus care about transmissions?" "Yes," I said. "He cares about every area of your life. You can ask Jesus for wisdom to know how to work on each transmission." He was a mechanic and knew that if Jesus healed him, maybe Jesus could help him at his job. He was stunned. He thanked me, picked up his items and headed out the door. As he walked through the automatic door, he yelled again, "WOW!"

I laughed, glancing at the worker behind the counter who was smiling. I love praying for the sick. It is FUN!

17

EVERYDAY ABUNDANT LIFE DECLARATIONS

Death and life are in the power of the tongue (Proverbs 18:21). Yes, your tongue has power. Speak these out loud on a regular basis and watch your life change for the better.

Today I am being transformed by the renewing of my mind with the Word of God. I put on the full armor of God: the helmet of salvation, the breastplate of righteousness, the belt of truth, and my feet are fitted with shoes of peace. I pick up the shield of faith, and the sword, which is the Word of God. I am holy and blameless in His sight. I have a power source within me, which is able to do abundantly beyond all that I could ask, think or imagine. Jesus Christ is in me. He is that power source!

I have the mind of Christ. I am a temple of God in which the Spirit of God dwells. I can do all things through Him who strengthens me. I have been raised with Christ and I seek those things which are above. All my sin was paid in full on the cross. I have died and my life is hidden with Christ in God. I have put on the new self, which is being renewed in knowledge in the image of the Creator.

When I speak according to the Word and will of God, heaven responds. I ask and receive. I seek and find. I knock and the door is opened unto me. I am in Christ and Christ is in me. For God has not given me a spirit of fear, but of power and love and a sound mind. Nothing is impossible with God. When I lay hands on the sick, they will recover.

May the words of my mouth and the meditation of my heart be pleasing in your sight, O Lord, My Rock and Redeemer! As I think, so am I. Today I will set my mind on things above, not on earthly things. I will think on things that are true, noble, just, pure, lovely, admirable, anything excellent and praiseworthy. I will think on such things. I am a doer of the Word of God, not a hearer only. Greater is He that is in me, than he that is in the world.

No weapon formed against me shall prosper. Whatever I do prospers for I am like a tree planted by rivers of water. I take the shield of faith and quench every fiery dart that the wicked one brings against me. I am more than a conqueror. God is fighting for me. I have the victory through Jesus.

Exodus 14:14; Psalm 1:3; 19:14; Proverbs 23:7; Isaiah 54:17; Matthew

7:7; 19:26; Mark 16:18; Romans 5:8; 8:37; 12:1-2; 1 Corinthians 2:16; 6:19; 15:57; Galatians 2:20; Ephesians 6:10-18; 3:20; Philippians 4:8; 4:13; Colossians 1:22; 1:27; 3:1-3; 3:10; 2 Timothy 1:7; James 1:22; 1 Peter 4:11; 1 John 4:4

18

DECLARATIONS FOR BUSINESS OWNERS

Declare a thing and it shall be established (Job 22:28).

Our business is God's business and God's business always prospers. I trust in the Lord and whatever we do prospers. All our ways please the Lord. We give Jesus all the praise, honor, and glory for what He is doing with our business. We are blessed so that we can bless others. We are vessels for the Kingdom.

No weapon formed against us shall prosper. We plead the blood of Jesus over this business and us. We can do all things through Christ who gives us strength.

God sends out the angels to the north, south, east, and west to get the people we need to buy our products. Favor surrounds us like a shield. The Lord goes before us and behind us with every step. We dedicate this business to the Lord. The Lord orders our steps.

We ask the Lord to bring us divine meetings with the right people that work for us and do great work. We love Jesus, and He will cause us to inherit wealth and fill our treasuries.

We ask for wisdom and knowledge when we are making decisions. We have the mind of Christ. From our mouth flows wisdom and our lips bring forth what is right.

We are strong in the Lord and the power of His might. Our sleep will be sweet as we are involved in this business.

The windows of heaven are open over us and God rebukes the devourer for our sake because we are tithers. The Lord has commanded us to be blessed; therefore, we are blessed and cannot be cursed. We are the head and not the tail; we are above only and not beneath. We will lend and not borrow.

God is Jehovah-Jireh, our Provider. We worship and adore Him. Thank you, Lord, for all you have done and all that you are going to do. You get all the glory! We receive everything that God has to offer us. We will be a blessing to others as we are blessed. We are a blessing magnet. Blessings are attracted to our business. Thank you, Jesus.

Genesis 12:2; 22:14; Numbers 23:20; Deuteronomy 28:1-14; 2 Samuel 7:29; Psalm 1:3; 5:12; 37:23; 103:20; 139:5; Proverbs 1:7; 3:24; 8:21; 10:31; 28:25; Isaiah 54:17; Malachi 3:10; 1 Corinthians 2:16; Ephesians 6:10; Philippians 4:13; 2 Timothy 2:21; Hebrews 13:12; James 1:5; Jude 1:25, Revelation 4:11

Living on the Road

19

WHO YOU ARE IN CHRIST

I can do all things through Christ who gives me strength. Each day I am renewing my mind as I meditate on the Word of God. I am a new creation in Christ. Old things have passed away. I am the light of the world and the salt of the earth. I am seated in heavenly places in Christ and I can come boldly to the throne of grace.

I am a child of God. Jesus has given me authority to do the things he did and even greater things when I believe His Word. Signs and wonders follow me. In the name of Jesus, I cast out demons, speak in new tongues and when I lay hands on the sick, they will recover. I love the Lord with all my heart and with all my soul and with all my mind and with all my strength.

I am saved by grace through faith. I am forgiven as I repent for my sins. I am delivered from all darkness in my life. I dwell in the secret place of the Most High and abide in the shadow of the Almighty. I cast all my cares on Jesus because he cares for me. I call to Jesus and He answers me. He turns his ear to me and I will call on him as long as I live. I am an heir of God and a joint heir with Jesus. I have eternal life waiting for me.

I am blessed coming in and blessed going out. I am the head and not the tail ending up on the top not the bottom in every area of my life. I am blessed with every spiritual blessing. I am made alive together with Christ. I am strong in the Lord and in the power of His might.

I am the redeemed of the Lord and the Spirit of God leads me. The Holy Spirit dwells in me because I am God's temple. When I am brokenhearted, the Lord is close to me. My God supplies all my needs according to His great riches in glory. He will never leave me or forsake me. The Lord goes before me and is always with me. I am strong and courageous. All things are possible because I believe the Word of God.

Deuteronomy 28:6; 31:6-8; Joshua 1:8; Psalm 34:18; 91:1; 107:2; 116:2; Jeremiah 33:3; Matthew 3:2; 5:13-14; 6:14; 19:26; Mark 16:17; 12:30; Luke 10:19; John 14:12; Romans 12:2; 8:17; 1 Corinthians 3:16; 2 Corinthians 5:17; Galatians 3:26; Ephesians 1:3; 2:5-6; 2:8; 6:10; Philippians 4:13; 4:19; Colossians 1:13; Hebrews 4:16; 1 Peter 5:7; 1 John 5:11

20

HEALING DECLARATIONS

Speak these out loud to increase your faith about healing.

I can do all things through Christ who gives me strength. I can do everything that He said I can do including laying hands on the sick and casting out demons. I have the power of God living on the inside of me. Jesus gave me all authority to trample on serpents and scorpions and over the power of the enemy. Nothing will harm me. I will lay hands on the sick and they will recover. The Bible says I can do what Jesus did and even greater. I believe for the impossible. I am bold as a lion when I sense that others around me need healing.

When Christ ascended, the Holy Spirit came to the earth. He is with me. He is my helper, comforter, and counselor. I trust in Him for guidance when I believe for healing.

Let the weak say, "I am strong." God has not given me a spirit of fear, but of power, love and a sound mind. By the stripes of Jesus, I am healed and whole. With long life God will satisfy me and show me His salvation.

The thief comes to kill, steal and destroy but Jesus came so I that can have life, enjoy it, and live abundantly in every area of my life. I am more than an overcomer by the blood of the Lamb. When I am in trouble or distress, I call to the Lord and He saves me. He sends His Word, heals me, and delivers me from defeat and destruction.

I praise the Lord with my mind, will, and emotions. I do not forget His benefits. He forgives me, heals all my diseases, redeems my life from the pit, and crowns me with loving kindness and tender mercies. He satisfies my mouth with good things and renews my youth like the eagles.

I am not moved by what I see or do not see when I pray for the sick. I walk by faith.

Psalm 86:7; 91:16; 107:20; 103:1-5; Proverbs 3:5; 28:1; Isaiah 9:6; 53:5; Joel 3:10; Matthew 19:26; 28:18; Mark 16:17-18; Luke 10:19; John 10:10; 14:12; 16:13; Romans 8:37; 2 Corinthians 1:3; 5:7; Philippians 4:13; 2 Timothy 1:7; Hebrews 13:6; 1 John 4:4

21

DECLARATIONS FOR CHILDREN

Children are a blessing from the Lord. The fruit of the womb is His reward. They are like arrows in the hand of a warrior. As for me and my house, we will serve the Lord. All my children shall be taught of the Lord and great shall be their peace. I train my children up in the way of the Lord.

My children are known for their actions. I decree an excellent spirit found in them. They honor their parents and they will have a long life on earth. They walk in integrity and in truth.

Lord, establish and keep them in your Kingdom so they will be rooted and grounded in your Word. Strengthen them in faith and may they be overflowing with thankfulness.

I decree that the Spirit of the Lord will rest on my children. The spirit of wisdom and understanding is being released to them. The spirit of counsel and might rest on them in all seasons.

I pray that they seek the Lord and His righteousness. May they hunger for things that pertain to Jesus and run after them. He equips them with every good work. The Lord has placed gifts and talents in them and I pray that my children use them for His glory.

May my children carry out God's perfect will for them. I declare they will accomplish that which is well pleasing in God's sight. He will complete the work that He has begun in their lives. May the words of their mouths and the meditation of their hearts be pleasing to the Lord.

Their names are written on the palms of God's hand. I release them to Him to do a mighty work. God has good plans for all my children. He has hope for them and orders their steps. God leads and guides them into their destiny that has been set before time began. God wishes above all things that my children prosper and live in health. My children will prosper in their mind, will and emotions.

God knows my children. He knit them together in the womb. The day each one was born He said, "They are mine." I dedicate them to the Lord and release them from any holdings that I have on them that would hinder them from seeking the

Lord and His perfect will. They are yours, Lord!

Joshua 24:15; Psalm 15:2; 18:30; 19:14; 37:23; 127:3-5; 139:13; Proverbs 20:11; 22:6; Isaiah 11:2; 43:1; 46:10; 49:16; 54:13; Jeremiah 29:11; Matthew 6:33; Ephesians 3:17; 6:2-3; Philippians 1:6; Colossians 2:7; I Thessalonians 5:18; 2 Timothy 3:17; 1 Peter 4:10; 3 John 2:1

22

AWESOME DESTINATIONS

For five years, we traveled the roads of the great United States of America as a family. Our average stay was three months in any particular area. When you live in an RV, you cannot spend money on "things" because there is no place to put them. So, we spent our money on sightseeing. With each new "home" we found fun things to do and interesting places to visit them. Included below are some of the BEST places we visited. Hopefully, you can enjoy them too. Happy Travels!

Texas

The Alamo	www.thealamo.org
AT&T Stadium	www.attstadium.com
Fort Worth Stockyards	www.fortworthstockyards.org
San Antonio River Walk	www.thesanantonioriverwalk.com

Louisiana

Church of the King   www.churchoftheking.com

Missouri

Branson Music Shows	www.branson.com
Dixie Stampede	www.dixiestampede.com
The Dutton's	www.theduttons.com
Faith Life Church	www.flcbranson.org
Sight & Sound Theater	www.sight-sound.com
Silver Dollar City	www.silverdollarcity.com
Victory Christian Church	www.victorycolumbia.com

Alabama

Calvary Assembly of God	www.calvaryassembly.org
Hot Air Balloon Festival	www.alabamajubilee.net
Point Mallard RV Park	www.pointmallardpark.com
Point Mallard Waterpark	www.pointmallardpark.com
US Space & Rocket Center	www.rocketcenter.com

Tennessee (we never lived here but visited it often)

Chattanooga Aquarium	www.tnaqua.org
Gatlinburg Sky Lift	www.gatlinburgskylift.com
Graceland	www.graceland.com
Incline Railroad	www.ridetheincline.com
Memphis Zoo	www.memphiszoo.org
Ocoee Zip line Adventure	www.Ocoeezipz.com
Rock City	www.seerockcity.com
Ruby Falls	www.rubyfalls.com

Ohio

Clear Waterpark and RV Park	www.akroncantonjellystone.com
Faith Family Church	www.myfaithfamily.com
Heini's Amish Cheese Factory	www.heinis.com
Hartville Market	www.hartvillemarketplace.com
Letterboxing	www.letterboxing.org
Niagara Falls	www.niagarafallsusa.org

Kentucky

Dinosaur World	www.dinosaurworld.com
Mammoth Cave	www.nps.gov

Georgia

Madison Church of God	www.madisonchurchofgod.com
New Life Church	www.newlifeeverday.com
Paula Deen's Restaurant	www.ladyandsons.com
Stone Mountain	www.stonemountainpark.com
Tybee Island	www.tybeeisland.com
Zoo Atlanta	www.zooatlanta.org

Mississippi

Jellystone RV Park	www.memphisjellystone.com

Arkansas

Agape Church	www.agapechurch.com
Buckstaff Bath House	www.buckstaffbaths.com
Balloon Festival	www.hotsprings.org
Little Rock Zoo	www.littlerockzoo.com

Arizona

Grand Canyon	www.grandcanyon.com
House of Healing	www.hardcorechristanity.com
Phoenix Zoo	www.phoenixzoo.org
Sedona Red Rocks	www.visitsedona.com
XP Ministries	www.xpministries.com

About the Author

Debbie lives an active lifestyle now that she is free from back issues. She enjoys hiking the mountains in Phoenix to spend time alone with the Lord. She ministers healing and deliverance to individuals. She mentors young women in her home on a monthly basis and teaches classes on how to lay hands on the sick both to adults and children. She lives in Arizona with her amazing husband and two beautiful daughters.

Connect with Debbie

www.healinglikeJesus.com
Debbie Hudspeth on facebook
healinglikeJesus@gmail.com
@debbiehudspeth on Instagram

Made in the USA
San Bernardino, CA
16 February 2017